I WILL ALWAYS BE IMMENSELY MERI (LOVING) YOU

Searching for the Balance of Ma'at

A Novel

Ra'ShyAlah Sakura the Poet

(Paul Mark)

Copyright © 2024 by Paul Mark

West Hartford, CT 06110

Printed and Bound in the United States of America

Published by:
Kemetic Nation Publishing
West Hartford, CT
markpaul36@yahoo.com

Packaging/Consulting
Professional Publishing House
1425 W. Manchester Ave. Ste B
Los Angeles, California 90047
323-750-3592
Email: professionalpublishinghouse@yahoo.com
www.professionalpublishinghouse.com

Cover Design: TWA Solutions
First Printing February, 2024
10 9 8 7 6 5 4 3 2

ISBN 979-8-218-36651-3

Publisher's note

For inquiries contact: markpaul36@yahoo.com

Dedications

I dedicate this book to my Mother (The woman that placed the love of God into my heart) Laura Brevard Mark and Father Alfred Mark, my heartbeat Queen wife Paula Mark, my daughter (Universal Star Blessing) Fana Marie Fahari Mark, my sister Jennifer Mark, (that always believed in me), my brother Abdulqadir Ali (Titus Mark), my niece Nia Mark (Nia Forever Faithful), my brother Johathan Mark, my cousins/sisters Keifa Mark and Kemba Mark, my Mark Family,(aunts, uncles and cousins), my Brevard family (aunts, uncles and cousins) my Bowen Family, my Rainey family and my new family, the Finch Family, my brothers from another mother, Thomas Jackson and Charles Trevor Joiner, to all the Political Prisoners held in the dungeons within the United States of America and abroad, to all my Warrior Ancestors that struggled for my and your spiritual freedom.

"Freedom must not be a construct of words to speak
of liberation. Liberation of freedom must always
be a constant fight for the revolutionary DNA that
exists in each of our Spiritual Souls!"

-Ra'ShyAlah Sakura the Poet

Table of Contents

Chapter One

You Are My Blessings of the Sopdets (Stars),
Created By Lah (Moon)

Baraka and Lyah Asari-Dokubo displayed remarkable strength as they worked hard to build a family of their own, even in the face of adversity. Lyah experienced two heartbreaking miscarriages in just three years, and she also had to contend with an irregular menstrual cycle, which worsened inflammation and affected her white blood cell tissue. To understand her condition better, Lyah's doctor conducted tests on her white blood cells and diagnosed her with polycystic ovary syndrome (PCOS). As Lyah immersed herself in extensive research on PCOS, her increasing knowledge left her feeling overwhelmed with panic and anxiety. Determined to find the best holistic doula in New York City, she conducted thorough research to guide her on her journey.

After interviewing eleven holistic doulas in seven months, Lyah finally found a holistic doula named Faith Abongo, whom she felt confident could assist her throughout her pregnancy.

Baraka, Lyah's devoted husband, consistently offered unwavering support, as Lyah maintained a positive spirit throughout the months. She diligently prayed to Neter, the Most High Creator, seeking complete healing over her womb to give birth to a healthy baby in the future. Lyah walked through Uptown Harlem with boundless enthusiasm, striking up cheerful conversations with family, friends, and even strangers she crossed paths with on the street corners. Lyah's impeccable fashion sense and her captivating smile were impossible to overlook. Wherever she went in the city, her contagious laughter echoed through the streets, a testament to her unyielding faith in Neter and herself.

May 19, 2020, became a memorable day for Lyah and Baraka when they went to Lyah's regular check-up with her OB/GYN. During the appointment, the doctor performed various tests, and the wonderful news emerged that Lyah was six weeks pregnant. Filled with overwhelming joy, Lyah and Baraka leaped from their chairs, their hearts (Jb) overflowing with excitement, and celebrated the moment with passionate kisses. Their profound love, referred to as "meri" in the Kemetic language, fueled their determination to embark on this journey once more.

Three months after discovering her pregnancy, Lyah and Baraka eagerly anticipated the day when they would finally get to embrace their baby boy, Mutulu Diara Asari-Dokubo. Each day, they diligently made preparations for his arrival. They started their mornings with a Ra (sun) rise morning prayer before going to work.

Chapter Two

I Will Not Ask For Your Forgiveness For My Past

On September 2, 2020, at 5:22 p.m., Lyah arrived at her home on 148th Street in the historical Sugar Hill on Amsterdam Avenue in Harlem, New York. Lyah looked up to the sky, smiling, saying a prayer as she rubbed her ankh necklace around her neck. She searched deeper into the sky, staring deep into the heavens, blowing love kisses to Ra (sun) before opening the front door of her brownstone home. She exhaled a deep breath, excited to arrive home from the long subway ride from working at her job in an exclusive boutique clothing store in Jamaica, Queens.

Feeling tired, Lyah entered the master bedroom she shared with her husband, Baraka. With a feeling of exhaustion, she carefully took off her high-heeled shoes and settled onto the bed, closing her eyes for a much-needed rest. After a peaceful nap that lasted twenty-six minutes, Lyah woke up and made her way to the bathroom, where she refreshed herself by washing her hands with soap and water. Taking a deep breath, she went to the kitchen, where she lovingly prepared dinner for herself, Baraka, and their precious unborn son, cradled within her sacred Universal Nu (Black) womb.

Rubbing her protruding belly, she talked to her prince. "Mutulu, are you hungry? I am going to make a halal lasagna dish with a garden salad. We need to hurry up and start cooking, because your daddy will be home soon from working a double shift."

One hour and forty-eight minutes later, Lyah finished cooking her homemade oven halal lasagna, leaving the food in the oven, and placing the garden salad in the refrigerator. Entering the living room, she turned on the stereo, and the room filled with the soothing sounds of smooth jazz. Lyah settled onto the couch and lost herself in the enchanting melodies. After about ten minutes, she gradually closed her eyes, drifting into a peaceful nap.

Less than an hour later, Baraka came home, unlocked the front door, and found Lyah peacefully asleep on the couch. The delightful aroma from the kitchen greeted him. He quietly opened the closet in the hallway, pulled out a neatly folded denim blanket, brought it to her, and carefully placed it over Lyah to ensure her comfort. Baraka patiently waited for her to wake up, eager to prepare dinner for both of them. About twenty-two minutes later, Lyah slowly opened her eyes, only to see Baraka looking at her with a heartwarming smile.

She reached out to him. "Ungawa (Black Power), my king. How was work today? I hope they didn't work you too hard, my king?"

"Ungawa! Grand rising, my queen. You know how it goes. I still had a great day at work. How was your day, the most beautiful Lyah?"

Lyah greeted Baraka with a warm smile and stretched her arms out to him, inviting him closer. Baraka responded with a mischievous grin and playfully shook his head, teasingly declining her invitation. However, Lyah remained determined, persistently reaching out for his meri (loving) embrace. "Baby, stop playing and come over here to me?"

Standing up, Baraka blew a tender kiss to Lyah and made his way to the kitchen. Soon, he reappeared, carrying plates of delicious food for both Lyah and himself. Settling on the soft area floor rug, Baraka lovingly fed Lyah her portion, attentively ensuring she enjoyed each bite. Once Lyah had finished her meal, he then proceeded to savor his own, occasionally sharing affectionate words with her as they dined together.

"My queen, the food is so delicious."

"My pleasure to serve you, my king. There is more lasagna and salad in the kitchen if you desire seconds."

"I like that you play jazz music while we eat."

"Art is the music that reflects light, that creates life. Music reflects the energy of the souls of people; spirits of their wiliness to reclaim their self-expression of their divine meaning of liberation."

After thoroughly enjoying his first serving of lasagna, Baraka headed back to the kitchen, eager to savor a second plate of food. When he finished the last bite, he leaned in and gave Lyah's soft, sweet lips a tender kiss. He then settled on the floor next to her while she reclined on the couch, showering her with affection.

Following their satisfying dinner, Baraka got up and moved through each room of the house, opening all the windows to let in the refreshing outside breeze. Meanwhile, Lyah remained comfortably nestled on the couch, gently caressing her protruding belly. When Baraka returned to the living room, he placed a pillow on the floor and sat beside Lyah as she lay on the couch. They both embraced the melodic jazz music playing from the stereo and the lively ambiance of Harlem coming in through the living room window.

Lyah softly said to him, "My great-grandmother Elizabeth Bey-El would set me on her knees and tell me stories of the Harlem Renaissance, and how she and her sisters would get up early to the rise of Ra (sun), leaving their home, running into the street, playing games with their friends that lived on 110th and 155th on Seventh Avenue. She would stare into my eyes with a sparkle in her eyes, saying with a giggle in her voice, calling herself a 'Harlem girl, born and bred.' Her father, Elder James Bey, introduced her to iconic theater producer and director Cornelius Coleridge 'Dick' Campbell when she was five years old. She talked about when she was younger, she would go to the American Negro Theatre founded by Frederick O'Neal to see theatre plays. Great-grandmother Elizabeth Bey-El told me she paid fifty cents to see a theatrical play seating in the balcony to watch Paul Robeson preform a magnificent performance. My great-grandmother told me every day was like a fashion show, watching people walk outside of their homes in their finest and sharpest clothes and fur coats. Every day was filled with adventure living in Harlem, watching people hustling to achieve their dreams. She called the community she grew up in 'The Children of Original Phenomenal Harlemites."

Baraka looked at her, and said, "My siblings, cousins and I are the fourteenth generation of native New Yorkers in my family. Every time I show my great Uncle Alfred Mark pictures I have taken of Harlem, he always tells me African people's presence must never be misinterpreted in Harlem, Brooklyn, and Seneca Village (modern day Central Park in Upper West Side neighborhood in Manhattan)."

In the seventeen century a Free African farming community that was residing in North of New Amsterdam that Black people built homes and businesses that were surrounded around modern day Greenwich Village South of Houston Street and Washington Square Park. Our ancestors continued building communities in the early nineteenth century with Seneca Village. Seneca Village is another prime example of our lineage to the shores of North America.

"Baraka, our history is our spiritual connection through the waters, trees, bricks, and each step our ancestors sailed and built to create a home on the island of New York. The more my parents and the elders of my family taught me about our family linage, tracing back to Senegal and Mali in West Africa to their voyages to the Western Hemisphere of the

Americas, I gain a greater understanding of my purpose to the Universe. When our ancestors created a new home for themselves, intermarrying with the indigenous Tonawanda and Wecquageek people that were originally from Kemet and Kush, they created and built communities throughout the Hudson River."

Smiling, Baraka nodded. "Our ancestors are the true indigenous descendants of the island of Manhattan. Over five hundred and nineteen Black women, Black men and children are buried in Seneca Village. Their graves are deep within the soil of Central Park. Many of my ancestors owned homes and business property in Seneca Village and modern day Wall Street in the eighteenth century. Many of them were victimized and suffered and were deprived with disenfranchisement by local governmental officials. Several families refuse to leave their homes and businesses in Seneca Village. My ancestors: William Rainey, Odesser Rainey, Johnsie Rainey, Charles Jonier and Thomas Jackson refused to leave their homes and businesses as they were creating their own form of Black Wall Street in Seneca Village (Central Park in Manhattan). Several families met their demise and was murdered by their corrupt white neighbors and white politicians. The remains of their bodies are under the monument within Duane Street."

Tears welled up in Lyah's eyes as she contemplated the deep pain rooted in her soul because of the domestic terrorism her ancestors endured. Baraka held Lyah in a tight embrace, offering comfort through his presence. Lyah went on to share her thoughts and feelings with Baraka. "Our relatives in lower Manhattan were buried under modern day Wall Street. Our ancestors were indigenous to the land before Europeans called this island we are living on Manhattan. In the eighteenth century and ninteenth century my ancestors built and honored this land as their home. Long before the Dutch and British thought by burying our ancestors their savage barbarism will be erased."

Baraka said, "Our families' linages to the island of Manhattan is scattered and buried underneath Manhattan and Brooklyn expanding long before 1492. Centuries of our ancestors suffering continued. Many of my ancestors were killed in the massacre of the New York City draft riot in July 1863. Several of my ancestors were forced to move to East New York (Brooklyn) or be massacred by new invaders that arrived from Europe. Our ancestors ran to safe places. One of the places was the historical Weekville neighborhood founded by a great Black man named James Weeks from Virginia that moved to Brooklyn, New York, after leaving Virginia. James Weeks established the land called Weeksville around 1838. When the New York City Draft Riots of 1863 began to reshape areas of Manhattan, more Black families living in Manhattan searched for a safe haven in Weeksville, in modern day neighborhood of Crown Heights, Brooklyn."

"Baraka, we should visit the African Burial National Monument in Manhattan next week."

"Most definitely."

"We can go to a theatrical play after we visit the African Burial National Monument, yes?"

"That will be nice to see a play after visiting the African Burial National Monument. One of my fondest memories with my other great-grandmother Rebecca Gordon was when she'd told me stories when I was a little girl about 2225 Lafayette Theatre on 132nd Street and Seventh Avenue. I wish I'd had enough money in 2013 to prevent it from being demolished."

"My great uncle Alfred Mark always talked about growing up throughout the Harlem Renaissance. Uncle Alfred would tell me when he was younger, he'd buy a ticket to watch a play before walking around Lafayette to feel the spirits of the great people that passed through the Lafayette Theatre. He'd tell me how captivated he was by the theatrical and professionalism of actresses and actors: Rosetta LeNoire, Ossie Davis. Ruby Dee, Paul Robeson, Josephine Baker, Bill Robinson, Bessie Smith, Adelaide Hall, Richard Bruce Nugent, and Rose McClendon."

"I cried when they demolished the Lafayette Theatre."

"Lyah, one of the millions of things I meri (love) about you is your Ka (soul). You have an old ka. I am so excited we are on the move, my Black queen, to having a family of our own!"

"I meri you always, my king Baraka!"

The lah (moon) arrived into the night. Baraka carried Lyah in his arms into their master bedroom, laying her on the bed. He began playing with her by tickling Lyah's feet as he kissed her ankh bracelet that was on her left ankle. Lyah start laughing as she kissed and licked the center of his forehead. They passionately started making intimate love throughout the night. They overslept the next morning, missing a doctor's appointment, sleeping in each other arms. Waking up around 10:10 a.m., they stared into each other's eyes.

Chapter Three

I Am More Than Who You See Inside of Me

Lyah and Baraka made it a routine to attend childbirth classes every Wednesday night at 8:00 pm to improve their knowledge and skills related to healthy pregnancies and childbirth. Over time, Baraka grew concerned about Lyah's heavy workload at the boutique, which appeared to be causing her high blood pressure. To combat this, Lyah turned to music as a way to relax and lower her blood pressure during stressful moments at work. Her passion for music continued to grow, resonating deep within her.

Each morning, she started her day with the beats of hip-hop and R&B, joyfully dancing to their rhythms before preparing for work. After working a ten-hour shift, Lyah would return home and engage in additional exercises around the house, as well as take walks in her neighborhood. She used to attend yoga classes from Monday to Thursday, striving to maintain a healthier lifestyle for both herself and her baby.

On September 28, 2020, Baraka and Lyah went out for dinner to celebrate their third wedding anniversary with a feast at their favorite soul food restaurant in Staten Island that served the best smooth strawberry drink, coconut yams, glazed blueberry cornbread, smoked turkey, collard greens, and peach cobbler. After dinner, they exchanged anniversary gifts. Baraka stared into Lyah's eyes, amazed that his Ka (soul) was falling deeper in love with Lyah's heart as she opened her anniversary gift. Thirty minutes later, they walked outside the restaurant, holding hands, feeling a cool breeze, as they waited for a taxi to take them home. When they arrived home, opening the front door, Lyah kissed Baraka softly on his lips, requesting he give her a back and foot massage with almond oil.

Every day, Lyah prayed for her baby's strength, struggling to push away the memories of her past miscarriages that threatened her confidence as she prepared for a healthy birth in the upcoming months.

On October 22, 2020, Lyah had a scheduled appointment with her obstetrician-gynecologist, Dr. Knox. He carefully examined her baby's ultrasound, ensuring there were no concerns. Dr. Knox assured her that the ultrasound showed normal development without any detectable medical issues. Leaving the appointment, Lyah stepped outside, feeling the cool breeze on her face before donning her coat and scarf. She took a deep breath, wearing a smile that expressed her newfound confidence in delivering a healthy baby boy.

A week later, on October 29, 2020, Lyah woke up from an afternoon nap, feeling the stress of her third trimester.

As she stood up, she unexpectedly felt sharp pains in her uterus and abdomen. She walked around her home, hoping to ease the discomfort. Concerningly, the abdominal pain was accompanied by frequent bleeding. Worried, she reached out to Baraka at work, explaining her pain. Baraka advised Lyah to contact her holistic doula, Faith Abongo, who assured him she would be fine before ending the call.

Lyah followed Faith's advice and went to the hospital immediately to determine the cause of her pain. At the hospital's emergency room, she was promptly transferred to labor and delivery.

Meanwhile, after Baraka spoke with Lyah, he found it difficult to concentrate at work. Overwhelmed with worry, he left his job abruptly and rushed home, taking the C-train in Brooklyn and then the number two subway train to their brownstone home on West 131st Street in Harlem, thinking Lyah was there.

Upon arriving home, their neighbor informed Baraka that paramedics had already taken Lyah to the hospital. Baraka sprinted to the hospital, his pace quickening with every breath, his mind solely focused on Lyah's well-being and the safety of their baby. Sweat streamed down his face as he passed each block. Finally, he reached the hospital's emergency room, feeling frantic. He approached Gloria Flores-Cruz, a nurse with a rich Puerto Rican heritage, hailing from Loiza, Puerto Rico. Baraka sought updates on Lyah's condition.

Loiza, a town in northeastern Puerto Rico, north of Canovanas and east of Carolina, traced its origins to runaway Africans, known as Cimarrones, who were brought to Puerto Rico by Spanish slavers. These Africans were intended to serve as slaves within the colony of Puerto Rico.

Many of the Cimarrones decided to reclaim their birthright of independence of freedom in the 1600s. They fought their Spaniard slavers by killing many of them before running away to freedom, creating a unified allegiance with other Africans as they founded Loiza, Puerto Rico. Loiza remained, to this day, the largest African community of descendants in Puerto Rico who had maintained their historical and cultural ties to their African ancestors from Loiza.

Gloria Flores-Cruz was a proud Nuyorican who held an abundance of pride in her Puerto Rican heritage. Her family had been living in New York City for three generations and counting. Gloria Flores-Cruz sat at the triage nurse's desk in front of a hospital computer in the emergency department.

With a concerning tone in his voice, Baraka asked Gloria to look up his wife's location within the hospital on her computer, worried for his wife's and his future prince's well-being.

Gloria Flores-Cruz asked Baraka to spell his wife name slowly.

"My wife's first name is spelled L-y-a-h. Her last name is spelled A-s-a-r-i-D-o-k-u-b-o. Lyah Asari-Dokubo. Please tell me Lyah and our son are healthy."

Gloria Flores-Cruz looked up Lyah Asari-Dokubo location within the hospital database system on the computer with a smile on her face. She ordered a nurse assistant to escort Baraka to labor and delivery. Gloria looked at Baraka with a smile on her face, saying to him in Spanish, "*Papa, felicidades a ti y tu esposa!*" ("Daddy, congratulations to you and your wife!")

Baraka looked into her eyes. "*Gracias*, mama."

"Once again, congratulation to you and your wife for the birth of your newborn baby. My nurse assistant will escort you to be with your wife and son."

Chapter Four

*The Rise of the Ra (Sun) Brings Forth a
Rebirth of Meri (Love)*

"Lyah," said Dr. Knox, his expression grave after running tests and examining her uterus, "I'm deeply saddened to share this heartbreaking news, but your baby has passed away in your womb. This occurred just a few hours before your arrival at the hospital."

Lyah's heart sank as the weight of those words settled upon her. Her thoughts raced, and tears welled up in her eyes as she struggled to grasp the enormity of what she had just heard. "No... No, that can't be true," Lyah whispered, her voice quivering.

"I truly wish it weren't true, but I'm afraid it is. Given the circumstances, we must take immediate action to ensure your well-being. The amount of blood you've lost is quite significant, and I strongly recommend emergency surgery to prevent further complications."

Lyah's breath caught in her throat. Surgery? The word loomed large in her mind, adding to her distress. "How much blood have I lost?" she asked, her voice barely audible.

Dr. Knox's expression grew more serious. "You've lost about a quarter of your blood. If we don't proceed with surgery promptly to stop the bleeding, there's a risk that your life could be in jeopardy."

Lyah's eyes widened in shock, and the room appeared to blur as the weight of the situation pressed upon her. She cast a gaze at her belly, where a whirlwind of emotions churned inside her. Fear, grief, and an overpowering determination to survive for her own sake and for the baby she had lost.

As the preparations for surgery began, Lyah shifted her focus to the monumental task ahead. She understood that she needed to summon the strength to push through, not just for herself but for the precious life she was about to bring into the world. Lyah exerted every ounce of her being, her silent struggle a testament to her resilience and indomitable spirit.

Amidst pain, sorrow, and a whirlwind of emotions, Lyah's determination remained unwavering. The room resonated with her efforts, each push bringing her closer to delivering Mutulu.

Lyah's body was soaked in sweat, every fiber exhausted from the ordeal of bringing her son, Mutulu Diara Asari-Dokubo, into the world through her Universal Womb. Her strength had been drained, and as she lay on the hospital bed, the memory of the childbirth pain was still vivid, mingling with the poignant realization that her son had been born stillborn. The room was filled with her moans and tears, breaking the silence.

Finally, Baraka reached the hospital room designated for Lyah. His heart swelled with anticipation, thinking he was about to embrace his new role as a father. With a mix of excitement and apprehension, he pushed the door open, but his smile faded as he took in the scene before him. Lyah, tears streaming down her face, shared a profound sorrow that seemed to envelop the room.

"Lyah." Baraka's voice was gentle, his concern evident as he approached her bedside. "What happened? Is everything alright?"

Lyah's eyes met his, filled with a pain that words could barely convey. "Baraka," she managed to say, her voice trembling, "our son... Mutulu..."

Baraka's heart sank, his breath catching in his throat as the weight of her words settled in. A wave of helplessness washed over him, a profound feeling of powerlessness in the face of such a heartbreaking reality.

As he witnessed Lyah's anguished state, Baraka's own emotions swirled within him—a mix of sadness, confusion, and a deep ache for his wife's suffering. He longed to shield her, to shield them both, from the crushing weight of this loss.

Without uttering a word, he moved to her side, gently draping a hospital blanket over her, attempting to offer some comfort. His hands trembled as he reached out to wipe away her tears, his heart breaking at the sight of her pain.

Lyah looked at him, her eyes reflecting the grief they both shared. "Baraka," she whispered, her voice fragile, "he was born stillborn... I couldn't... I tried..."

Tears welled up in Baraka's eyes, his vision blurring as he fought to contain his own overwhelming sorrow. He leaned in, resting his forehead against hers, their tears mingling in their shared grief.

As the weight of the moment settled upon them, Baraka stepped out of the room, gently closing the door behind him, the echoes of Lyah's cries seeming to linger in his ears. He sank to the floor, silent sobs wracking his body. He pounded his fists against the cold, unfeeling surface, the physical pain somehow reflecting the emotional turmoil surging within him.

In those moments of raw vulnerability, Baraka mourned not only the loss of his son but also the shattered dreams and hopes that had accompanied Mutulu's journey into the world. His cries blended with Lyah's in a lament of mourning, an expression of their shared heartbreak in the face of an unimaginable loss.

Baraka stands up, steps outside with tears in his eyes, and starts taking deep breaths, trying to contain the pain in his soul. He closes his eyes, inhales the fresh breeze, and feels emotionally drained, thinking about the loss of his son, Mutulu.

After twenty-three agonizing minutes, Baraka reentered Lyah's assigned hospital room, his heart shattered but his emotions carefully hidden from her. As he stepped into the room, he found Lyah's medical nurse bringing Mutulu to her. Lyah extended her arms, her eyes fixed on Mutulu's tiny face as she cradled him in her embrace. Tenderly, she stroked Mutulu's cheek, her gaze then lifting to meet Baraka's.

With a mixture of sadness and determination in her eyes, she softly spoke to him, her voice a whisper in the stillness of the room. "Baraka, he's so handsome." She kissed Mutulu's lips. "He looks so peaceful. They are lying to us, Baraka. I prayed and prayed for Mutulu to be born healthy. No, no Baraka, our baby, Multulu, didn't die in my womb. Mutulu is just sleeping. He cannot leave us now. We need him so much! Please tell me, Baraka, he's alive. Mutulu is alive! Please tell me, Baraka!'

Baraka hugged and kissed Lyah, consoling her as she placed Her right hand on her universal womb, holding Mutulu against her chest. With the death of their son, Mutulu Diara Asari-Dokubo, each tear Lyah and Baraka cried, shattered their broken souls. Throughout the night, Baraka stayed by Lyah's side, placing a seat on the left side of Lyah's bed, holding her hands as she couldn't sleep.

After a few hours of giving them time to grieve their loss, Dr. Knox entered the room, observing the pain etched in Lyah's and Baraka's eyes.

Dr. Knox steadied himself, inhaling deeply before a faint smile appeared as he addressed them. "I wish I could've saved your son."

However, Baraka's gaze sharpened with anger, his frustration at odds with the doctor's seemingly detached demeanor. He interrupted Dr. Knox, his tone intense yet strained. "Our son has a name."

"I understand you are in pain now."

"No, you don't understand. How are you going to say from the side of your neck, you understand my pain! You don't even know our son's name. Our son's name is Mutulu Diara Asari-Dokubo!"

"Sir, I did everything I could do to save your son, Mutulu Diara Asari-Dokubo. I am sorry for your loss."

"Nah, I don't want that. You hold onto that for yourself!'

Baraka's frustration escalated, his anger boiling over. Driven by a storm of emotions, Baraka runs towards Dr. Knox, tears welling in his eyes. He gripped Dr. Knox's neck, his fingers tightening with a mixture of sorrow and rage. "You killed my son. You killed my prince! Why did you kill my prince? He was my linage to the future!"

The room was charged with the strength of his emotions. Baraka's grasp on Dr. Knox's neck was a frantic effort to express the profoundness of his sorrow. His words were a direct outpouring of agony, a mourning for the life that had slipped away and the hopes that had been shattered.

Hospital security guards rushed into the room, pulling Baraka off of Dr. Knox, who knew Baraka was reacting out of pain. Dr. Knox walked out of the room. Heather C. Hill, the labor and delivery/maternity nurse manager urged Dr. Knox to call the police to ensure Baraka was arrested for physically attacking him without justification.

Dr. Knox refused to press criminal charges against Baraka.

Baraka wiped away his tears, swallowing the pain that was on the verge of making him cry. He looked over at Lyah, resolute in his determination to keep his own suffering in check and to be her source of support. He walked over to her and sat down in a chair beside her, gently but firmly taking hold of her hands. Their eyes met, conveying an unspoken agreement and determination between them.

"Lyah," he began softly, his voice laced with a quiet determination, "we'll get through this together."

Lyah locked eyes with him, her gaze holding a blend of sadness and thankfulness. She squeezed his hand back, finding solace in his touch amid the chaos. "Thank you, my king. I don't know how I'd manage without you."

Hours drifted away, the burden of time's passage visible on their faces, forever connected by their shared grief. It was three hours and sixteen minutes later when the door to Lyah's hospital room swung open, and in walked Dr. Knox, accompanied by an unexpected group of four hospital security guards.

Baraka made an effort to collect himself and stepped forward to confront Dr. Knox. He reached out his hand, a sign of goodwill amid the tension in the room. "I apologize for my outburst earlier. It was a lot to handle, and I appreciate your efforts."

Dr. Knox's eyes softened, his handshake firm as he

acknowledged Baraka's words. "I understand. Emotions can be overwhelming in these situations. Thank you for your understanding."

Baraka nodded, then gestured to Lyah, his expression a mix of curiosity and concern. "What's happening?"

Dr. Knox took a deep breath, his gaze shifting between them before he began to explain. "I needed to follow up and clarify some aspects of Lyah's case. During my examination, I had to ensure her safety was paramount. Unfortunately, the diagnosis for your son is that he was stillborn."

Baraka's heart sank at the confirmation, the words cutting through him like a blade. He turned to Lyah, his eyes meeting hers, sharing a world of emotions that words couldn't convey.

Lyah's voice was soft but resolute as she addressed Dr. Knox, her eyes glistening with unshed tears. "Thank you for doing what you could, Dr. Knox. We appreciate your efforts."

Dr. Knox nodded, a mixture of compassion and professionalism in his gaze. "I'm truly sorry for your loss. If you have any questions or need support, please don't hesitate to reach out."

As Dr. Knox left, the room felt heavy with the weight of their grief. Baraka turned back to Lyah, his voice a hushed murmur. "Lyah, we'll remember Mutulu. He was a part of us, no matter how brief."

Lyah nodded, tears finally escaping down her cheeks. "I know, and we'll get through this, just like we always have."

United in their pain, they clung to each other, finding solace in their shared journey toward healing.

Chapter Five

Akhu of Ma'at

Lyah and Baraka buried their hearts (Jb) in a private service in their Ka (souls), denying their pain and regrets of the past to each other. Sociologically they are in two different directions from one another refusing to surrender their hearts (Jb) to the consequence of the shattered vision of love as husband and wife.

After spending a night at the hospital with Lyah, Baraka became overwhelmed with anxiety. He left the hospital and returned back to work. After working a double shift, he then returned home to analyze his next move.

Days passed by since Lyah gave birth to her son. Still in the hospital, she tossed and turned in her bed, pondering if her husband meri (love) her the same in the future after receiving the devastating news that their beloved, Mutulu, born stillborn.

Two days later, Lyah's doctor discharged her from the hospital. She came home, entering their bedroom and glancing around, the space now haunted by memories of the day she had lost Mutulu.

On November 6, 2020, at 11:14 a.m., three days after Lyah had returned home, she was suddenly seized by intense abdominal pain. She felt a growing desperation and repeatedly tried to reach Baraka on his cellphone while he was at work, seeking his help. Unfortunately, Baraka's phone went unanswered as he dealt with his work responsibilities.

Four hours later, Baraka finally made it back home. As he entered the front door and stepped into the hallway, he was greeted by a scene of distress. There was Lyah, lying face down on the hallway floor, reminiscent of her previous ordeal. Her hands clutched her belly, and a trail of blood formed a stark contrast against the floor. Fear and urgency propelled Baraka forward. Without a second thought, he rushed to her side, his heart pounding in his chest. Kneeling down beside her, he gathered Lyah into his arms, his touch gentle yet urgent, his voice a mixture of concern and reassurance.

"Lyah, I'm here. It's going to be okay. I've got you," Baraka murmured, his words a lifeline in the midst of their shared turmoil. He held her close, a protective embrace that sought to shield her from the pain and fear that enveloped them both.

Lyah looked up at Baraka. "Baraka, where were you? I've been calling you all day!"

"I was at work."

Baraka immediately rushed Lyah to the hospital. She lay in the hospital bed for days, contemplating her future with Baraka after they previously suffered two miscarriages and

Mutulu begin born stillborn all in the past two and a half years.

After working a long shift at work, Baraka made his way to the hospital to visit Lyah. He walked into her room with a bouquet of pink roses and handed them to her. While she accepted the flowers, Lyah couldn't help but notice that Baraka wasn't wearing his wedding ring. Nevertheless, he offered her a smile, his thoughts wandering to whether Lyah would find it in her heart to forgive him for the past. He had spent time with his friends in the streets and had even visited strip clubs with the extra money he had earned from his job.

Lyah and Baraka deny their pain and regrets of the past. Sociologically, they were in two different directions from one another. They both refused to surrender their hearts (Jb) to the consequences of yesterday and their future as husband and wife. Lyah stared at Baraka as he looked out the hospital room window.

"Grand rising, Lyah. Have you looked out of the window to see outside this morning?'

"Morning. No, I haven't looked out the window."

"I said grand rising to you."

"Morning."

"Lyah, the brightness of Ra (sun) is shining so magnificent this morning."

"I haven't notice."

"Lyah, I know you meri (love) the beauty of Ra shinning. You have to look at this breathtaking view of Harlem and the beautiful trees in the park near 135th Street. The beauty of the day reminds me when I was a seventeen-year-old, desiring to articulate the destiny of my purpose as a Kemet man (Black man). Many of my homies refused to see past the block, but I knew there was more to life than what the streets could offer me. I decided to wake up April 7, 2016, to stand up to walk toward my destiny. I searched for knowledge of self. When I planted my feet on the sacred grounds in Harlem on 135th Street and Malcolm X Boulevard, I visualized the path of my destiny. Each step led me to feel a deep responsibility as I walked through the front entrance of the Schomburg Center for Research in Black Culture."

Lyah continued staring at Baraka without saying a word to him.

Baraka faced Lyah. "Why are you looking at me that way?"

"How am I looking at you?"

"I am telling you about the day that change my life forever as I gained consciousness. I am sharing my experiences with you."

Lyah looked at Baraka with a deep mysterious stare in her eye. "I am listening to every word you are saying, Baraka."

"You're looking at me different. As if I am not your husband but a stranger in your presence."

"Yes, we are married. Sometime, when you look away while I am speaking to you, it makes me—" Lyah stopped speaking in mid-sentence, staring deeper into Baraka's eyes.

He looked away, not wanting Lyah to look into his eyes to know what his Ka (soul) was feeling.

Lyah continued. "Baraka, the last few days, I've wondered where your heart been? I don't know, Baraka, what you want from me anymore. Why are you hiding your eyes from me? Look at me, Baraka?"

"Lyah, what are you talking about? I am not avoiding from looking into your eyes. You are the one looking at me differently since—"

She interrupted him. 'You must have forgotten. I know your ways and how you think."

"All these different experiences has changed me from the fate of the consequences of each miscarriage and now knowing our baby was born stillborn..."

"I can recognize the difference in your personality and behavior, but answer this question that is buried in my Ka (soul). I don't understand how you allow the pain to distance yourself from me."

"You act like I left you. I am still here with you. I know you better than you think I do. We are a team; we are in this together. Did you call your parents to tell them about the baby being born stillborn?"

"No. Since my parents have been living on Martha's Vineyard the last year, I never told them I was pregnant this time. I was going to prepare a special festival to surprise them by inviting them to dinner when they return home to Harlem in the wintertime." She paused. "So no, I didn't tell my parents about—" Lyah couldn't say Mutulu's name. "I cannot bear the pain of telling my parents I lost their grandson forever by giving birth."

"Lyah, never forget we are in this together."

"The last miscarriage; I thought I'd never have to go through this devastation ever again. With the first two miscarriages and now knowing I gave birth to my baby being born stillborn. I am so confused. Why is this happening to me? I am left with more guilt in my heart, soul, and womb. Baraka, promise me when we leave the hospital, we'll never again speak of the miscarriages and the stillborn ever again. Promise me?"

Baraka sat next to Lyah, avoiding eye, wiping tears from her eyes. Kissing her hands, he laced his chin on the palm of her hands. "I promise we'll never talk about the miscarriages and our baby being stillborn. Lyah, how can I emotionally and physically support you through these difficult times?"

"I don't mean to be so difficult. I meri (love) you, Baraka. There is nothing you can do. My Jb (heart) already feels guilt after delivering our baby that was born stillborn."

Baraka turned his back, looking at his cellphone, texting someone in secrecy. *I already told you I'll be there after I leave the hospital.*

"Baraka? Baraka? Baraka, are you listening to me? Baraka who are you texting?"

"Uh, what were you saying? Lyah, we will have—"

Lyah interrupted him. "Don't say we will have our own family. Baraka, you said that the last miscarriage a year ago."

"You are still my wife; the destiny of tomorrow's desires will allow us to decide if we will continue our family as husband and wife with a newborn baby."

"Baraka, why do we have to endure so much pain?'

He continued texting the person on his cellphone, looking at pictures on his cellphone, smiling.

Lyah looked at him. "Baraka? Baraka? Baraka, are you listening to me? I feel so alone..." Lyah sighed, looking down at her belly with tears in her spirit and eyes, saying to herself, "Why is this happening to me over and over again? I am only twenty-five years old. I cannot endure any more devastation in my Jb (heart) and Ka (soul)" Then, she looked at Baraka and screamed, "I never want to ever talk about the two miscarriages or my baby being born stillborn ever again in my life!'

"Lyah, everything is going to work out."

"I don't want hear that! I cannot find peace when you are around me. Get out of my hospital room. I want to be alone."

"What! Now I am the problem? You straight buggin'."

"I am not playing. Baraka, you don't meri me. Get out of my room now!"

"Yo, I don't need this. I am out of here!"

Chapter Six

The Awakening of the Lah (Moon) and Ra (Sun)
Creates a Spiritual Resurrection of the Sopdets (Stars)

Four months had passed since Lyah and Baraka had tragically buried their prince, Mutulu. Baraka and Lyah moved around their house, isolating their Jb (hearts), only allowing their bodies to share the love of intimacy twice in the last four months. They both stood apart, destining their Jb (heart) not to look into each other's Ka (souls) too deeply, afraid of the consequence of their past pain.

On February 7, 2022, Lyah arrived at the Jamaica, Queens Station subway platform at Van Wyck. Overwhelmed by anxiety, she found a seat and couldn't contain her emotions, tears streaming down her face. Her Ka (heart) raced, and she sought solace through prayer to the Neter (Most High Creators), pleading for answers to her prayers. She was on a quest to find a holistic healer who could connect with her soul (Ka) and potentially assist in healing her womb for a healthier pregnancy and delivery. Despite the tears and prayers, Lyah's determination remained unwavering.

During this introspective moment, a woman in her mid-fifties, dressed in Afrocentric attire and a hairstyle celebrating her heritage, sat down beside Lyah. She looked at Lyah with empathy and understanding in her eyes.

"Hotep, my beautiful, young, Kemetic sister. I pray for a blessing upon your Ka (soul). Don't you know you are holistically anointed with a special secret gift?"

Lyah wiped her tears, looking up to meet the woman's friendly smile. They started talking, and soon their conversation turned into laughter. Lyah explained her troubles to the elder, sharing the reasons behind her pain.

During their chat, Lyah learned the woman was a certified holistic healer from Staten Island, New York. The elder, named Mrs. Kenya Ture, gave Lyah her business card, showing she genuinely cared about Lyah's well-being. Mrs. Kenya Ture also mentioned an appointment she had with another young woman in Mount Vernon, who faced a similar issue as Lyah. This gave Lyah hope; she wasn't alone.

Before Mrs. Kenya Ture got off the subway, she hugged Lyah tight, and whispered in her ear, "The Spirit of the Goddesses of fertility lives within your universal womb, my Kemetic sista Lyah. Call me as soon as you can to schedule an appointment. Young sista, always remember in your Ka (soul) you were born from an Ancient Mother and you will give birth to an Ancient scarce child!"

"Hotep, queen Elder Kenya Ture."

"Hotep, my beautiful golden sista. Until we met again."

Lyah had done extensive research on Mrs. Kenya Ture before she contacted her to schedule an appointment. All the women Mrs. Kenya Ture holistically healed notified Lyah of her dedication to help heal every woman she worked with to restore their health. Lyah and Mrs. Kenya Ture met at an organic health café in Staten Island. Mrs. Kenya Ture showed Lyah her qualification as a holistic healer that expanded over twenty-six years of experience and her certifications as a holistic healer. Mrs. Kenya Ture reassured Lyah's faith by empowering her Ka (soul).

"I can see in your eyes that the pain of the passing of your babies has affected the energy in your womb to give birth again." Mrs. Kenya Ture touched her hands with a tender touch from her soul. "Lyah, I am going to holistically help you to regain the power in your Universal Nu (Black) womb."

Lyah hired Mrs. Kenya Ture as her personal holistic healer to assist her holistically to cleanse her womb to restore a positive balance to increase a higher, healthier birth rate of fertility in the future. Mrs. Kenya Ture instructed Lyah to change her diet to reduce anti-inflammatory foods by eating healthier foods with natural organic soy seeds from the soil, foods with iron, inositol, probiotics, ginger, cinnamon, and calcium. Mrs. Kenya Ture instructed Lyah to eat more vegetables and take natural vitamins with herbs to help heal her womb, to increase her fertility.

Mrs. Kenya Ture encouraged Lyah daily that her Ka (soul) and body will be restored to her divine spiritual natural balance of complete health soon, telling Lyah, "Keep the faith of your spiritual channels flowing with the rejuvenation of propensity of alpha and omega."

Mrs. Kenya Ture continued to help heal Lyah's womb holistically, placing Lyah on a strict diet and detox to cleanse her womb, and teaching Lyah how to pray properly and meditate to relax her spirit, mind, and blood flow through her body.

"A Universal Nu (Black) woman's energy must always transform within the essence of her Ka (soul), spirit, and body to be empowered through the divine process of conception of her body. Through the birth of her baby and when her child or children give birth to their own children or children. Universal Nu (Black) woman's energy is always transforming to connect to always flowing through Neter."

Lyah tried her best to follow the advice and instructions given by Mrs. Kenya Ture to relax. However, sometimes, anxiety took over her thoughts. She kept thinking about what Baraka might be doing when he wasn't with her. She knew Baraka was handsome, had a charming personality, and could easily be flirty. He always dressed stylishly and had a strong sense of confidence, especially rooted in Harlem.

There were days when Lyah didn't see Baraka at all, and this made her wonder how faithful he was to their marriage. She thought about his intense and passionate nature, especially when it came to physical pleasure, given his traits as a Gemini man. Lyah's curiosity led her to call Baraka repeatedly during her work hours, as she wondered who might be fulfilling his need for intimacy and affection when she wasn't around.

Chapter Seven

The Birth of the Ra (Sun) is Setting in Your Eyes

Baraka came home after spending the entire night out. He used his right hand to unlock the front door, a camera bag slung around his left shoulder, carrying his Canon EOS-5d Mark IV digital SLR camera. Opening the first of two front doors, he entered and took a moment to glance around the living room. The sound of Lyah playing the song "Blessed Those Who Struggle" by The Last Poets filled the air.

With a sigh, Baraka lowered his head and unzipped his camera bag. Eager to relive the moments captured by his Nikon D750 FX format digital camera throughout the night, he immersed himself in reviewing the photos. Just then, the ringing of his cell phone interrupted his concentration. He balanced his camera gear and answered the call, simultaneously opening the second front door.

His focus shifted as he looked up and saw Lyah approaching. She questioned him about his whereabouts and the time, noting that it was already five forty-five in the morning. With a touch of irritation, Baraka responded,

"Pause, can't you see I'm on the phone, woman? Don't ask me where I've been. If you keep bothering me, I might just leave!"

Lyah caught the sound of a woman's voice coming from the other end of the phone line while Baraka was talking. The woman seemed excited upon hearing Baraka's voice and exclaimed, "Where are you, Raka?"

Baraka glanced at Lyah from the corner of his left eye as he stepped outside to continue his conversation with the woman. After a few minutes, he returned inside the house, slipping his cell phone into his right pant pocket. He deliberately avoided making eye contact with Lyah.

"Who was that woman calling you, Baraka? Does she know you are married?"

"She's just a friend from work."

"Okay, Baraka, if you going to leave every time we have a problem, maybe you should pack your stuff and turn back around and leave your house key and walk out the door and never come back. I'll help you pack!"

Baraka looked at Lyah. "What! I brought this brownstone before I met you, Lyah. This is my house. My ren (name) is on the deed. I placed your ren (name) on the deed after we got married, to ensure you know this house is yours as much as it is mine. I gave you a place to share with me."

"Baraka, I invested years into you. You better stop playing games with me! I don't know why I stay this long with you. You don't deserve me!"

"Lyah, stop talking at me and listen to me. Stop thinking you really know where I was last night!"

"Baraka, I'm listening."

Now irritated, Barak raised his voice. "I am tired. I work hard day and night. I am trying to make more money for the both of us, and you want to keep arguing with me every time I come home to find peace."

"I am not arguing with you. You think money can replace your presence in my Jb (heart)? You must not know me the way I thought you did. I don't need your money. I work, too. I have my own money."

"'Lyah, say less. I don't have time for your nagging today. Woman, you ain't ready to listen to me."

Baraka's cellphone began to ring once more. He retrieved it from his left pants pocket and glanced at the screen to see the caller's identity. Recognizing the telephone number, he turned his back and grasped the doorknob, preparing to exit through the front door. "I'll be back when you are ready to listen and stop thinking you can control me."

"I am not going to ask you again, Baraka. Who the hell have you been fucking?"

"Yo, you better stop coming at me. You are the only woman I need."

"I meri (love) you, Baraka, but I cannot carry this dying relationship moving in slow motion with fears and uncertainty. Baraka, you only running into the darkness where no one can save you. If you want me to continue meri (loving) you in my heart, stop leaving me every time I show you my vulnerability."

Baraka stood at the door with his back to her. "We used to say 'grand rising' to each other every morning when arising to face Ra (Sun). What happened to us, Lyah? When I am not here with you, I am working double shifts at my job every day to create a better life for you—"

"Baraka, where is your wedding ring?"

Baraka lifted his left hand, deliberately displaying it to Lyah. Resting on his wedding finger was his wedding band. Lyah's gaze followed his movement, her eyes focusing on Baraka's finger.

"I am surprised you are wearing your wedding band on your finger now because I know you take it off soon as you leave home."

"Stop talking to me like you know me! If you really know me, you wouldn't keep questioning me! How long are you going to hold the mistake against me for leaving my wedding ring home when I visited you in the hospital?"

"I've always been faithful to you, Baraka. What about the last time I was a patient in Harlem Hospital? Rather than comfort me when I need you most, you left me to go to the strip clubs to be with your homies to hang out with them, spending money you should've brought home."

"How many times do I have to keep apologizing to you? Since that day after you were discharged from the hospital, I stopped going to strip clubs. I admit I was wrong for leaving you all alone at the hospital. Lyah, I know I hurt you by lying, by telling you I was at work when I really was at a strip club.

Lyah, I apologized for leaving you by yourself. But since that day, I carried myself as a Kemetic man of integrity."

Lyah covered her face with her hands, feeling anxious as memories of her previous miscarriages surged through her mind. The painful images of losing her babies in her womb haunted her thoughts. She turned to Baraka, her eyes reflecting the hurt she felt, and spoke with a heavy heart. "I keep hearing a voice in my head. God is telling me I am not meant to be a mother. With my first miscarriage, I didn't know I was pregnant until I went to my physician's office because I was experiencing flu-like symptoms. He told me I was three and a half weeks pregnant. Before I could express joy at being pregnant, he told me I miscarried four days ago. In my first trimester. A few months later, I got pregnant again. I tried to erase each day of the memories of being pregnant, but my Ka (soul) reminds me every day. My second miscarriage I was in my second trimester."

"Lyah, I still remember the sound of you crying for days."

"I still don't believe I fully was able to grieve. I told myself that means I had to accept I had lost my baby again. The last one, delivering my baby that was born stillborn, devastated my Jb (heart). I was so close to finally giving birth and having my baby in my arms. My Jb (heart) shattered in pieces as my Ka (soul) remained silent. I am not a mother."

"Lyah, let's change the conversation. Last night, while I was walking the streets, focusing my camera lens on the pain, I witness that we as a people inflict on ourselves and each other. I stared into hundreds of our people, Kemet nu's (Black people) eyes, seeing the infuriation and vexatious in our Ka (souls). I closed my eyes, allowing my camera to speak through each picture I took. I opened my eyes, listening to the music of the city. I suddenly realized my camera was out of film. I bent down on one knee, looking into my camera bag for more film. Before I stood up, I placed my hands over my face, wishing to wash away our Kemet nu troubles and pain. I cannot change yours or my yesterday, but I know all the years of searching for meri have led me to you."

Lyah averted her gaze, avoiding direct eye contact with Baraka. He stepped nearer, positioning himself beside her, and gently rested his hand against her left cheek. In response, she shifted away from his touch.

"Baraka, don't touch me!"

"Lyah, I will continue honoring my wedding vows we made together."

"Hmm, okay."

"Sometimes you are emotionally cold toward me. I am done apologizing to you."

"I called you several times. Where were you? Lately, you have been ghosting me,"

"The extra time I do have to myself, I am moving around the city with my cameras. One day I want to live out my desires in my spirit to travel throughout the world using my cameras to explore the Universe to understand it better with my camera lens."

Lyah's gaze rested on him, uncertain of how to ease his pain as she observed the sorrow etched in his eyes.

Baraka looked at Lyah. "I am tired of hustling early in the morning to get my guap (slang word for money) up and moving around before Ra (sun) rises to go to work. Sometimes I wake up and cannot recognize my own face staring back at me in the mirror. I get dressed putting on my work uniform, feeling my body moving without my Ka (soul). I feel my body running to catch the subway. I do this routine every morning to go to work to make a few hundred dollars to make someone else's dreams come true to become a multi-millionaire. When I reach the subway station, taking several steps to go down to catch the subway, I stand on the subway platform, waiting for the subway to arrive, thinking I am only getting paid half of the work I do daily, knowing I am not mastering my own prudential. Lyah, one day I am going to quit my job and open my own photography and art school to help keep Kemet (Black) youth get off the streets that feel trapped and are killing each other, feeling their only way to survive the streets is to be a predator to prevent from being the prey. I want to help our people realize that with each death by another Black person, the ones pulling the triggers are killing themselves each time they kill another Black person. We must show our Kemet nu family another way out of the street game."

Lyah smiled, peering into Baraka's eyes. "Baraka, that sounds great."

"That's why I work so hard."

"Baraka, let me help you."

Baraka looked at Lyah, struggling to trust his Jb (heart) to heal within her Ka (soul). "No, Lyah, I don't need your help. I can do it by myself."

"Sometimes, Baraka, you act like you are the only one that sacrifices."

"All I do is work for you and me to have a better life. I am tired of you complaining about what I don't do for you. I need you to start appreciating the man that I am."

"I am tired of hearing your excuses for not doing better. I should be the one asking you to appreciate me. Baraka, be a real man and get yourself together!"

Baraka's cellphone began to ring once more. He silenced it by turning off the sound. Avoiding Lyah's gaze, he shifted his eyes away, intent on keeping his emotions hidden within his heart.

Meanwhile, Lyah directed her gaze toward him. "You never really appreciated me."

"Lyah, I haven't shown you how much I appreciate you?"

"Baraka, who keeps calling you?"

"My job is calling me to see if I can come into work tomorrow on my day off from work."

"I am not a foolish woman. Tell your jump-off to stop calling you when you're home with your wife."

"I see you standing in front of me, but your eyes are telling me you know where I've been and know what I am thinking right now."

"Baraka, I asked you a question?"

"Lyah, I already told you about questioning me about where I've been! You are my wife. There is no other woman. It's my job, calling me to ask me if I can come into work tomorrow on my day off from work!"

"Baraka, let me see your cellphone. I have to make a quick phone call."

"No. Why can't you use your own cellphone? You just want to see who was calling me!"

"Say less. I am tired of all your cheating and lies."

"Lyah, you don't trust me anymore. Go 'head, look at my cellphone. Go 'head! You are the only woman for me. No woman can replace you in my Jb (heart). Lyah, you have changed ever since we lost the babies."

"We promised each other to never mention what happened."

"Lyah, you have to start trusting me if we going to make this Akh (relationship) last."

"I have given the best of me to you, Baraka. One thing I cannot stand is when you lie to me. Baraka, you forgot how we first met. Baraka, don't lie to me. Be a man, a real man! Look me in my eyes and tell me the truth. I know you can never be faithful to just one woman!"

"You really believe I cannot be faithful to you?"

"If you're going to leave me for her, do it now and save my Jb (heart) from the embarrassment of telling you I meri you ever again."

"It's not about who I was in my past."

"So, what's her Ren (name) or are you going to keep that secret like so many other lies you keep hidden from me?"

"I am not lying to you, Lyah."

"Baraka, are you going to tell that other woman that you're sneaking into her bed in the middle of the night? You should know me better than that. I am a very intelligent and sophisticated woman. I don't share. You are my husband. I play for keeps."

"Lyah, here you go again, accusing me of cheating. I am tired of this. I already told you; you weren't listening. There is nobody else for me. If I am having a secret affair, it's with you, Lyah! Because you give me your body every night but run and hide your Jb (heart) from me when I try to share my Ka (soul) with you."

"Why should I trust you? Why?"

"I don't know why I am explaining myself to you, Lyah. I spent the hold night thinking about all the reasons I shouldn't come back to you."

"Say less, Baraka. I am done."

"You know what?"

"Say less. What happened to you, Baraka, saying less? Why are you saying more? You don't have to stay. I suspect you are going to leave, anyway."

"How do I, as a man, tell the truth to you if you always think I am lying to you? How do you know when I am lying, when you, Lyah, don't even trust your Ka (soul)? Lyah, I spent the whole night walking the streets thinking about you. Painting pictures of the multiple shades of my journey with each canvas, painting pieces of my Ka. It's hard for me to tell you how much I meri you. I walked around the streets in the middle of the night, painting pictures with my camera lens, trying to avoid thinking about my past and how meri has failed me so many times in the past."

"Baraka, in all your past Akh (relationships) before you met me, were you ever faithful?"

"I am not answering that question."

"That's okay. You just told me your answer."

"Before I met you, I never had a woman that gave me a reason to be faithful when I could just find another woman to provide me with a new experience."

"So, the answer is no. You never were faithful to any woman you've dated! How are we really going to make this marriage work if we both admit we don't trust meri?"

"I never said I don't trust meri."

"So, what are you saying?"

"Ever since we lost our prince Mutulu…—"

With a pained expression in her eyes, Lyah turned to distance herself from Baraka. She raised her hands in the air, gesturing in a way that interrupted him before he could finish his sentence.

He grabbed her left wrist. "Hold up?"

"I am not going to do this with you. Let go of me now, Baraka!"

"No. Not until you talk to me!"

"Oh, today you have time to talk to me. Where have you been the last few months when I needed you? Lately, you've been ghosting me. Where have you been when I needed you the most? Oh yeah, I forgot. You've been at the strip club. You better let go of me, Baraka, now before I start screaming!"

Baraka released his grip on Lyah's wrist. She walked away, and Baraka trailed behind her. She shouted at him to cease following her. In response, Baraka attempted to grasp her wrist once more, but she managed to evade his reach. He quickly moved to stand in front of her, locking eyes with her.

"We need to talk about our son?"

"You can talk to yourself because I am not doing this with you anymore."

"Lyah, I know you don't want to deal with the loss of our babies. The pain runs deep in my Ka (soul), but we need to heal to be able to have the strength to move forward."

"Baraka, you are not going to admit to me, but I know what you are thinking."

"Lyah, what are you talking about?"

Lyah's eyes welled up with tears, and eventually, tears cascaded down her cheeks. She gazed at Baraka; her emotions evident in her tear-filled eyes. "Every time I stare into your eyes, I know you blame me for the miscarriages and Mutulu being born stillborn."

"Lyah, no one is to blame for the miscarriages or Mutulu being born stillborn." He paused, shaking his head. "You have to stop torturing yourself for the death of our babies. You did your best to eat healthily and work with your personal holistic doula throughout your last pregnancy. Lyah, you aren't at fault for the miscarriages or Mutulu."

Lyah brushed the tears away from her eyes and drew in a deep breath, shaking her head slightly. I" don't want to cry anymore. The first miscarriage I was in my first trimester; I didn't know I was pregnant." Lyah felt overwhelmed with exhaustion and overcome with extreme pain in her Ka (soul) saying. "I don't want to talk about losing my babies anymore. I am so tire—"

Baraka pulled Lyah into his arms to comfort her.

Lyah looked at him. "What about the other women in your past? Baraka, please let go of me! We have so much to talk about before—"

Bending down on his knees, placing his arms around Lyah, he kissed her belly. "You need to stop looking back at my past to start having more faith in my spirit. I am telling you about my real feelings in my Jb (heart). You have to stop listening to your friends and that noise in your mind that's blocking your Jb (heart) from moving away from all the fears you buried in your mind. Lyah, you are right. We do have so much to talk about. Why are we talking about yesterday when we need to start over with a new beginning with today and tomorrow and forever the future we will share together? I meri you. If you don't believe me, I'll let your Ka (soul) and Jb (heart) decide how to meri me immensely after we explore our Ka (soul). We can reach higher with our meri with a kiss and the destiny we will share together. Lyah, when I look at you, I realize it's not all about me. When I look into your eyes, I see you really meri me, but sometimes I think to myself, what if—"

Lyah pulled away from Baraka and paced around the room. "What if what? You say that as if it's a bad thing to meri. What's wrong with meri?"

'Lyah, I do meri you, too, but I'm not ready to face meri alone attached to more pain, so I keep running away from my Jb (heart)."

"You need to free yourself from your foolish pride."

"Who you think you are talking to? Watch how you talk to me, Lyah! I am not a fool! What does foolish pride have to do with our future?"

"I don't know what to say to you. Do you want to continue on with this Akh (relationship)?"

"Yes, I do. You are beautiful, Lyah, you are radiant!"

Silence filled the room, greatly amplified by the energy radiating from Lyah as she moved around. Baraka picked up one of his cameras, adjusting the lens with precision, and marveled at how Lyah's statuesque and captivating elegance had ensnared his soul. He began taking pictures of Lyah, particularly focusing on her powerful structured eyes.

A knock at the door suddenly interrupted the stillness. Baraka's best friend, Omari Zawadi—where "Zawadi" means "gift" in Swahili—knocked on the front door. Baraka opened the door, extending a friendly fist bump as a greeting.

Omari Zawadi walked into the house. "Hotep, king. What's really good, Baraka? You ready to go, Mo (Uptown slang for friend)?"

Baraka looked at Omari. "Ungawa, Omari. What are you talking about?"

"Mo, come on. You didn't get my text message?"

"I am feeling that black diamond ankh necklace you are rocking, Omari! Yo, Mo, you want something to drink?"

"Most definitely."

Baraka walked into the kitchen while Omari approached Lyah and hugged her. "Hotep, beautiful. You look more stunning every time I see you. How are you doing?"

"Hotep, Omari. I am doing good. How are Keyshia and your pretty little girl, Olugbala, doing? How old is Olugbala now?"

"Keyshia and I had a birthday party for Olugbala. She just turned three years old last month."

"I was waiting for my invitation to Olugbala's birthday party."

"Lyah, you never needed an invitation to know you were invited to Olugbala birthday party. I grew up on 118 Street and you grew up on 119 Street. I look at you as my sister. My home is always open to you."

"Thank you. I don't have a brother, so I've always seen you like a brother since we were five years old."

"Wow, we've known each for a long time since we were five years old, Lyah. We are family."

"Wow, time passes by so fast. I can remember going to Keyshia's baby shower when she was seven and a half months pregnant with Olugbala."

"Lyah, remember you don't need an invitation to Olugbala's birthday party next year. You're my family. I consider you to be my sister. You know Keyshia and I had another baby girl two months ago? We Ren (named) her Shakur."

"I know, congratulations. I came over to your house two weeks ago to see baby Shakur. I also came over last Wednesday. When I came over on Wednesday to visit Keyshia, she told me I had just missed you. You left for work a few minutes before I arrived. Keyshia and I had a long conversation. When are you going to marry Keyshia?"

"Really? You going to talk about this now?"

Lyah smiled at Omari.

"Keyshia knows how I feel about her. We have an understanding."

"Since we all are family, what understanding is that?"

Omai paused, as if in deep thought. "Lyah, I consider you my sister, but that's between Keyshia and me. She is the mother of my two baby girls. We don't need a contract or a ring to prove our commitment to each other. Keyshia knows she doesn't need a ring; she will always be my wifey."

"Omari, what about making it official by making Keyshia your wife? She deserves to be called Mrs. Keyshia Zawadi."

"Here you go. My parents have been married for twenty-eight years. My parents are the most miserable married couple I know. Marriage or love? What goes first? Sometimes I wonder if marriage stops the Ka from finding the true existence of the true meaning of meri. My parents maybe loved each other at the beginning of the Akh (relationship), but I know they never meant to meri each other to create a forever meri. My parents are just waiting for my youngest brother, Ra'Keim, to graduate from high school to get a divorce."

"Your parents told you they are going to get a divorce after Ra'Keim graduates from high school?"

"Yes, my parents told me they are getting a divorce."

"They always seem happy to me."

"I am not surprised they are getting a divorce. Behind closed doors, there are some personal characteristic traits of ourselves we will never reveal to the public, that only close loved ones know about my parents. They are great parents to my siblings and me, but they are not good for each other."

"Your parents always seem like they were in love with each other every time I saw them together in public."

"I am twenty-seven years old; I cannot remember growing up ever seeing my parents kiss each other with passion for each other. When I was younger, I used to catch my mother from the corner of my eye, looking at my father with disgust on her face. That still goes on to this day, when I go to my parents' house to visit them. I still see my mother looking at my father with a strange look on her face. That's never going to be Keyshia and me. I meri Keyshia, she knows that. When Raka and I were facing twenty-five to life on torching and murder charges for three dudes that were murdered from Jamaica, Queens, New York, we had beef with over a revenge murder they did to our big homie's wife."

"Baraka still has nightmares over his time incarcerated in federal prison."

Omari Zawadi looked at Lyah with a deep stare, with pain in his heart. "Yeah, the alphabet terror squad of the United States government tried to take Baraka and my lives away for crimes we never committed."

"I know that changed your life forever, Omari, because Raka doesn't like reliving that time in his life."

"I remember we told our attorneys over and over we were innocent as he looked into Baraka's and my eyes, seeing only street dudes that killed Nu (Black) men cold bloodily over revenge for killing our big homie's wife. After months of trying to convince Raka and me to take a plea bargain because the prosecutor's attorney linked Baraka and me to four unsolved murder cases in the Bronx, our attorney notified us if we plead guilty to the murders in Jamaica, Queens, New York, the prosecutor was willing to offer sixteen to twenty-five years prison sentence if we testify against a suspected drug dealer from Soundview House Projects in the South Bronx. Baraka and I knew the streets had no mercy when death comes. We refused to cross-dress (snitch) to gain a lesser prison sentence.

"We moved around the prison yard with our heads held up high, knowing any day could be the last moment the air is sucked out of our lungs. If we close our eyes, thinking about a smile on someone's face as a friendly gesture of love or respect, we knew a death sentence with knives in our back and neck would've been our final demise. When the correctional officers would lock the prison walls at night, Baraka and I would go to our individual prison cells. When we were allowed out of our prison cells, we would go to the prison yard, walking by fake dudes with envious dumb smiles on their faces as they looked at Baraka and me, giving us head nods, saying, 'Whut up? Respect, my dudes.'"

Omari paused for a few seconds, contemplating the nightmares he had experienced in prison. "Many of our fake homies on the block that Baraka and I protected by going to war with rival street teams to save their lives, left us for die. As they listened to rumors in the streets, that Baraka and I were facing life sentences, they ghosted us when it came to any kind of support, counting down the days of our demise. All our support came from our bloodline family and our real, real street family. Those experiences changed me forever. I learn real quick betrayal comes from all different directions, from frenemies if the price or the revenge is enough. I could've died at any moment from the one most closest to me! I only slept certain hours at night while I was in prison. When I did fall asleep at night, I would sometimes choke from my tears falling from my eyes, feeling my heart beating in the streets!"

Omari paused for a brief moment, his thoughts dwelling on the nightmare he had endured during his time in prison. He then proceeded to share more about his prison experience.

"Baraka's father and my father are old-school revolutionaries, they sent us both commissary money and book copies of *The Education of Sonny Carson* by Mwina Imiri, Sonny Carson Abubadika, the book *Jailhouse Lawyers: Prisoners Defending Prisoners vs. the U.S.A.* by Mumia Abu-Jamal and Doctor Frances Cress Welsing book, *The Isis Papers: The Keys to the Colors*. Baraka and I read each book, restoring our faith in our spiritual and self-consciousness within our individual hearts. We continually did our own research to prove our innocence, remaining connected to the streets to sending messages keeping our names in the streets to our homies we will never cross dress. Our attorneys were finally convinced we are innocence after we force them to interview witnesses that were present at the time of the three dudes' murders.

"For months, the police refused to do a complete investigation to identify the real murders. Were the real killers arrested for the murders of the three dudes? No, the murder cases is hidden in the police department files. The police never really looked for the murderers only wanted Black bodies to be lynched and hung in the injustice. I mean, the justice system…

"All the government really wanted was Baraka and me to die imprisoned for capital murders that was unsolved. Raka and I remained in prison for months in federal penitentiary on false charges we were accused of for time we will never get back. It is sad what happened to those dudes, but no way Baraka and I could've murdered the three dudes in Jamaica, Queens. We were in Providence, Rhode Island, getting guap (money) when the murder took place. Raka and I refused to take plea bargains to get leniency. We decided to tell our attorneys to allow our cases to be tried by a jury to fight the charges.

"Baraka and I became more closer while we were incarcerated. Dudes in the yard knew we were unfamiliar to penitentiary codes of law, seeing us as fresh meat. We rep Uptown 118th and 129th Streets. When they touched Baraka, I told them they touched me and when they touched me, they touched Baraka. We had a few homies looking out for us a few times when we had to fight, but Baraka and I came hard with force with revenge with each person that touched us. Our knuckle and iron game was the only thing that allowed us to survive prison. We were all we had between life and death in prison. Those days were tough, but we strengthened our bond as brothers not cross dressing (snitching) to turn into federal bitches for a crime we both didn't commit."

Lyah looked at Omari. "Keyshia told me you remained strong while you were imprisoned."

"My baby, Keyshia, kept my head up. She came to each and every one of my court appearances. Standing by my side the whole time I was locked up. Keyshia is a real queen. She kept it tight the whole time I was locked up. She's a natural hustler; she came up with Baraka and my guap (money) bail the first time our bail was set before the judge increased the bail when other murder charges was placed on us. My baby, Keyshia, she's my Jb (heart).

"The last day of the trial, Baraka and I stood to our feet, scared, as we were sweating. We still tried not to show the fear we felt in our Jb (hearts) with our heads held high, hearing the jury reading each count of the charges we were charged with. I heard Baraka's and my family praying together as the jury foreman announced the jury verdict. Each charge we were found not guilty. When we were acquitted, I hugged my family one by one for believing in me. I then hugged and kissed my baby, Keyshia, telling her 'Thank you for holding me down. Hit a lick, I am always going to take care of you.' I don't know want I'd do without Keyshia. I wake up every morning and sometime in the middle of the night looking forward to kissing Keyshia when she's sleeping."

Lyah looked at Omari, smiled, and knew he really did love Keyshia. "Omari, were you afraid of getting married? Keyshia is my soul sister! I only ask because I cherish you and Keyshia so much."

"I'm not afraid of anything..." Omari paused and continued, "Lyah, we care about you deeply as well. I just don't want Keyshia and me to end up like my parents did, twenty-five years from now, wasting time without truly meri (loving) each other. Maybe my parents will finally find happiness when they go their separate ways.

"By the way, how is your grandmother doing? I was driving home two weeks ago, and I saw her waiting at the bus stop. I turned around to give her a ride home to Mount Vernon. She had me laughing the whole time during the ride, telling me how handsome I am. She even joked that if she were forty years younger, Keyshia would have some competition. When we reached her house's driveway, she hugged me so tightly, telling me to trust in my faith to the Most High into infinity. It was a warm and heartfelt embrace. Lyah, your grandmother recited a Kemetic prayer in praise of the Akhu.

"Praise to the Akhu, the blessing dead, hail the shining ones, my ancestors. You who have gone before me, I thank you for who I am and who I will become. Praise to the Akhu the beautiful west, appearing as gold in the belly of Nut, may I honor your name and wear your mantle with respect. You go where gods cannot. Praise to the Akhu, faithful companions standing in both worlds, your wisdom guides me if I but ask behold and accept my offering, may they be pleasing to you. Praise to the Akhu, loyal guardians, protecting me on my path, drive out evil before me and light my way, until we meet again in the field of reeds."

Omari Zawadi looked at Lyah. "When I was moving in darkness on the block, I felt like I was wearing the lion skin of my revolutionary hero. Tupac Amaru Shakur in my Ka (soul). Feeling like me against the world. I was always thorough, making sure no one ever knew my next move so they could penetrate my Jb (heart) in the streets. Both of my grandmothers transcended before my birth. No elder ever prayed for me with great abundance and conviction. She placed her hands on my chest, touching my Jb (heart). Your grandmother is very special to me. She gave me four ankh necklaces for Keyshia, our two daughters and me. That day I really didn't want to let her go. How is your grandmother doing?"

"She had the flu for the past few days but when I want to her house before going to work yesterday, she told me she is starting to feel better. We have plans to have a late lunch together next Tuesday."

"What time next Tuesday?"

"Around 3:30 p.m."

Omari smiled, looking Lyah up and down. "Lyah, when are you and Baraka going to have a baby? Lyah, you ain't getting no younger?"

"Boy, please, I am only twenty-six years old. I am still young. Baraka and I will not have children until our businesses start flourishing."

"You serious?"

"Yes, I am. I am not going to have children until I open my second bouquet shop."

Omari Zawadi looked at Lyah. "Alright, you better stop waiting for the perfect timing."

"Whatever, Omari. Say less."

"Cool, do you, Lyah. I cannot wait for your grandmother to meet Keyshia and our baby girls! Every time I see your grandmother, she always asks me when she will meet Keyshia, Olugbala and Shakur. It's too late now, but I have to call your grandmother tomorrow morning to find out if she is feeling better. I am going to see if she needs me to bring her anything from the organic health store on 126th Street before I go to work tomorrow. Lyah, you still have my math (cellphone number)?"

"Unless you changed your number, I still have your cellphone number."

"I still have the same number. Lyah, don't forget to call or text me the address of the restaurant. I'll treat everyone. I am going to bring my queen Keyshia and my two little pretty baby girls."

"I'll bring my little niece Ashayt (Kemetic name meaning "She who possesses abundance") as a playmate for your two little princesses. I'll ask Baraka if he wants to come."

Baraka returned to the living room, a cold drink for Omari held in his right hand. He handed the drink over to Omari.

After a few sips, Omari said to Baraka, "I was just talking to Lyah about our time in the pen. Yo Mo, do you remember those dudes hating on us when we were in the cage, in the penitentiary?"

Baraka replied, "Yo Ox, I try not to think about that hell cage."

"Mo, I remember dudes hating on the way you were moving, spending time with your natural charm and charisma with those female COs (correctional officers)."

"My father taught me when I was growing up to always maneuver time by standing in my square as a king! Never show fear or envy around my enemies, while I am moving forward to get to the queen."

"Every day we had to watch our front, back and side from death."

"We walked the prison yard keeping a safe distance to maintaining our self-preservation from the prison guards and other prisoners."

"I still think about how you parlayed those female COs to give you whatever you wanted. I still have battle scars from the work we put in those prison walls. We lost some battles fighting, but most of the time we laid our bricks from our fist on those who questioned how thorough our knuckle game was. Ayo it was meant for us to win, we made soundtracks of our lives on the streets when we were growing up!"

"No cap I don't need nobody hollering my name or making a movie of my life. My body of work in the streets is the movie! No clout chasing. I am just specking facts!"

"Hard body if anyone been on the streets as long as we were wiping blood from our tears, they know some stories should never be repeated to civilians with glass tongues (snitching)!"

"Omari it's not our fault that when most dudes were born, they slid out of their mother's wombs. We stepped out of our mother's womb born as kings!"

"Yo, Baraka you ready?" Omari whispered into Baraka left ear. "Ayo, the homies and me are going to cruise a few strip clubs tonight. We going to get lit and turn it up at the strip on Matthew Street."

"Mo (Uptown slang for friend), I am feeling that new big boy joint (trunk) you got parked outside. Yo, I can't go out tonight; I am going to spend the night with my queen."

"Mo (Uptown slang for friend), you can't be serious. We are each other right hand man, hard body. You know I don't trust anybody but you, since we got back home from the penitentiary. I need you to watch my back from these crab ass suckers?"

"Omari, you are my brother for life. We will always be brothers for life but I need to mellow out from running the streets so I can be with my goddess."

"You are going to miss seeing Pebbles. She no longer dances at Black Diamond strip club. She dances now at Jewell strip Club. Pebbles been asking about you the last few months. If you don't hurry up and smash that I going to take your place. Baraka, air and opportunity is the only things that separates me from smashing Pebbles. Homie real soon I am going to suck up all the air in the room for me to shoot my shot and smashing Pebble taking her to a hotel room."

Baraka hugged Omari. "No cap…hard body, son. Since I've been trying to deepen my Akh (relationship) with Lyah,

I realize I must make changes in my life. Homie, we all have to make choices in our lives one day soon. to face the consequences to choose the choices to be our path in life. Hotep, warrior."

"Hotep to you. I am on the move, warrior. Let me straighten out my black diamond Ankh chain necklace."

"Ayo, I really mean that king. Omari, go home to your queen and two little princesses. Omari, you are as close to me as my right lung. Be conscious of your decisions. Hotep, warrior."

Omari hugged Lyah before leaving, then gave Baraka a manly hug before walking out the front door to return to his vehicle. He contemplated whether he should drive to Jewell Strip Club or go home to be with his family. Omari kissed his Ankh black diamond chain necklace, hearing the deity Tehuti speaking to him in the wind. "When all of your thoughts, feelings and actions reflect the word of God then the power of God's Spirit and a peace that nothing can challenge that flows through your Being."

Chapter Eight

*You are the Most Highest Creator Blessing to
My Ka (Soul)*

Lyah watched Omari as he walked outside and got into his big boy joint (truck). She stared out of the living room window, watching Omari as he sat in his vehicle, contemplating his next move. Eventually, Omari drove off in his vehicle. Lyah turned around from the window and said to Baraka.

"Baraka, why were you and Omari so secretive when you all were talking? Did you tell Omari about the miscarriages?"

"No, I didn't tell him about the miscarriages. Omari and I are brothers; we always create a cypher building through our experiences over our wins and taking some losses together."

"I meri Omari, but he better not be trying to play reckless impetuous games. Keisha's all-in to meri (loving) him. She's really in-meri with Omari."

"I am sure Omari will do the right thing."

"He better."

"Big homie will do the right thing at the end of the day."

"Baraka, I want you to be totally honest with me, are you truly ready to meri me completely?"

"Most definitely. I am serious about always meri you, Lyah!"

"Baraka, tell the truth. Are you still cheating on me?"

Baraka looked away, not wanting Lyah to know how angry he had felt about her constant questioning regarding whether he was cheating on her.

"Are you serious! Listen, I can't keep doing this with you all the time. Self-esteem must be inherited, not given!"

"What are you talking about! I've always had confidence in myself. I never needed you to build up my self-esteem, never!"

"Why do you keep asking me if I am cheating on you? I keep telling you, I've always been faithful to you! Do you want me to tell you I am cheating on you? I am tired of you asking me the same question over and over while I deal with all this stress, trying to maintain my sanity as a powerful and strong Kemetic (Black) man in a society that is trying to exterminate me every day! Stop looking into my past to see the man I used to be! I am going to say this for the final time! No, I am not cheating on you! I have never cheated on you, never!"

"Baraka, you proclaim to be a Kemetic man, I need you to tell me the truth! Did you stop cheating on me with all those strippers that you gave half of your check to?"

"Lyah, I am not going to flex on you."

"Baraka, all I want you to do is be honest with me."

"I never cheated with a stripper or any other woman."

"You might not be cheating now, but did you stop cheating when you got caught or just recently? Your history proves you are a womanizer!"

Baraka rubbed his hands together, taking a deep breath. "I take my faith and beliefs of Kemeticism seriously. When did I ever get caught cheating on you? That's the problem with you—you keep bringing up my past relationships before I met you in this house, causing problems in our Akh (relationship). You better stop using my past to avoid working on healing your own insecurities. Before we got married, I knew I shouldn't have told you about my past relationships because all you do is throw them in my face."

"Baraka, I am only stating the facts – you are a womanizer."

"Lyah, you keep asking me more questions to avoid answering my questions."

"What do you want to ask me?"

"Since we lost our—"

Lyah interrupted Baraka to prevent him from completing his sentence, walked down the hallway into her private designer room, and locked the door. She looked over her fashion décor designs. Baraka followed after her, attempting to open the door, and noticed that Lyah had locked it. He began banging on the door, demanding she open it so they could continue conversing. Lyah refused to open the door to speak with him. Baraka attempted to speak with Lyah through the wooden door that separated him from her.

Baraka banged in the door. "Lyah, open the door so we can finish this conversation."

"No. I have designs to complete. I already told you; I am not doing this with you today. We promised we'll never talk about what happened ever again."

"How long are you going to hide in there?"

"I am not hiding; I have work to do."

"Lyah, we have to stop acting like we can avoid dealing with the trouble in our Akh. I am trying to be here for you so we both can heal, but you keep hiding yourself from me."

"Baraka, you promised me that after I lost my babies, you'd never talk about my miscarriages or my baby being stillborn. I already told you; I don't want you to ever mention it ever again."

Baraka raised his voice as he continued banging on the door out of frustration, continually talking to Lyah through the door. "Lyah, you weren't the only one who lost our babies."

"I carried my last baby, Mutulu, for eight months and sixteen days, enduring the torment of hours of bleeding, only to be told by an OB/GYN physician, while I lay in my assigned hospital bed, that my baby was born without any signs of life! I was the one who had to give birth, knowing my baby, Mutulu, had died in my Universal womb, not you. You can never compare my hurt and pain to yours, Baraka!

"I looked to my side, seeing my holistic doula, knowing she wasn't to blame for me losing my baby. I blamed myself for my baby's death. My holistic doula bent over, hugging me, telling me that I was going to get through this. I thought to myself, 'I will never, ever get through this horrific pain.' I lay in the bed as my Ka (soul) cried, moaning the death of my baby boy, Mutulu. I felt my holistic doula's tears and my own tears rolling down my face and neck. Refusing to believe the Neter (Most High Creator) would allow my womb to forsake me again, letting me give birth to my baby that was born stillborn!"

"Lyah, I never left your side during the time you were in the hospital. Lyah, don't forget I was by your bedside, holding your hands in the hospital the whole time we lost our prince Mutulu."

"Yeah, I know you always came to check on me in-between going to work and going to the strip clubs."

"I apologize for any neglect I showed you, Lyah."

"Baraka, why didn't Mutulu's Spirit want to come through me?"

"I don't have an answer, I don't know. Some people say broken hearts have a hard time flying. But I say broken hearts have a hard time dying, wishing they were meri. Mutulu's Spirit will return through your Universal Womb again. Come on Lyah, I meri you. Please open the door?"

Lyah whispered under her breath to Baraka, "I meri you too, but I refuse to confuse meri, fears, and sex, thinking that the hurt will go away by ignoring the pain that exists in our experiences together."

"Baraka, I meri you more than you are willing to ever meri me."

"Hold up, Lyah, what are you talking about? I thought we were talking about the loss of our baby Mutulu. What do you want from me? You know I meri you and will do anything for you."

"You are doing way too much right now. Don't say you meri me unless you really mean what you are saying."

Baraka started laughing out of frustration, shaking his head as he walked away from the door. "Ayo, say less. I am done with this."

"I knew you'd eventually leave, Baraka!"

Chapter Nine

*I Am Resting My Jb (Heart) Inside of the
Lah (Moon) Spirit*

Weeks went by as Lyah had refused to communicate or look directly into Baraka's eyes. She would go to work every morning from Monday through Friday and come home, sleeping in her designer room at night. Baraka would sleep alone in their master bedroom.

One night, Baraka lay in bed, tossing and turning. He attempted to sleep but couldn't calm his mind. He stood up, walked to the master bathroom, and took a shower. After returning to his bedroom and drying himself, he opened the bedroom closet door and hung his wet clothes on a hanger. Then, he proceeded to take out a designer white dress shirt and designer black jeans from his closet. He dressed and looked at himself in the mirror, grabbing his camera bag before leaving the house through the front door without letting Lyah know he was going.

Baraka walked around and saw his comrades, Kevin, Jay, and Erik, hanging out on the block. He approached them, giving each of them a black fist and pound (a form of a handshake with a person's fist balled up). Twelve minutes later, Omari drove up to them on the block.

Baraka asked Omari, 'Ayo, what are you doing out here?"

"Yeah, Keyshia's too tired to cook. She got me out here looking for a restaurant that serves some good food."

"Where are you trying to go?"

"I don't know, Black man. Baraka, I thought you were chilling with your queen?"

"Nah, I need a break from all that drama she's kicking my way."

Baraka, Omari, Kevin, Jay, and Erik surrounded each other, building a cipher of wisdom, sharing knowledge like fire to empower the circle they were creating.

Kevin looked at Omari and asked him. "Omari, are you Caribbean? You look Caribbean."

"Nah, I am not Caribbean. Kevin are you Caribbean?"

"Yes, I am Caribbean. My mother's side of the family is from Saint Kitts, but I grew up in Barbados."

"Big ups and much respect to all my Caribbean brothers and sisters. Kevin, while growing up, I spent a lot of my summers in Staten Island. My family roots are spread throughout the islands of New York. My bloodline's history in the islands goes way back to the 1400s, dating back to the creation of Manhattan Island. Baraka and my family were one of the hundreds of original families that built Seneca Village (modern-day Central Park in Manhattan, New York City) in the early 1800s. My family was forced to escape for their lives from Seneca Village in the 1860s, moving to Weeksville in Brooklyn, modern-day Crown Heights, Brooklyn, and Staten Island's historical Sandy Ground section. In the early 1900s, my father's side of the family reunited with many of my destined relatives when they moved to Uptown Harlem. Many of my family members still live on Staten Island."

Baraka looked at Omari and smiled. "A lot of Nu people (Black people) don't know our history to the city/island we call New York. Our history is not buried. Our history is alive in our Ka (souls), Jb (hearts), and bloodline."

"Word up, King!"

"I know a lot of African-Americans are moving back to the South to rediscover their roots—"

Jay interrupted Baraka. "You're bugging. Some people are moving to the South for a better life for themselves and their children. What's wrong with that? I am thinking about moving to the ATL myself if things don't get better soon."

"Yo, Jay, you ain't listening to me. Don't ever disrespect me or interrupt my wisdom when I am kicking knowledge! Listen to me carefully. I respect native Moorish (Black) people's decisions to create better lives by going down South. I am spitting facts about our hidden journey. Our ancestors built with their blood, sweat, and suffering, and their graves are marked with many of the blueprints that show how the

South was built through the slavery of African people—a holocaust through the Atlantic trade of African slaves that brought our ancestors from north to south and from south to north. Once again, I respect Moorish people's decisions to move wherever they want to go. But for me and mine, I am not going anywhere! My roots are here in the Islands of New York!"

Baraka looked at Omari with a smile. "Word, that goes for me too, warrior king. Our ancestors planted seeds in the soil and built every one of these bricks surrounding the islands. Our ancestors in the seventeenth century fought on both sides of The Revolutionary War – for the Loyalists and Patriots – to be free from the bondage of servitude. They also fought to prevent their children from being sold down the river during The Revolutionary War from 1775 to 1783, ensuring they would never be reclassified as slaves."

Erik looked at Baraka and Omari, his face expressing bewilderment. "Ayo, I didn't know how much our people helped to create and manufacture the United States of America and throughout the Americas. When my family and I came to the United States, we were told Black Americans were lazy and rapist criminals that are only on governmental welfare assistance. The more I learned and researched, I realized that it's lies to separate Kemetic Nu from uniting around the world!"

Baraka looked at everyone gathered around in the cipher. "Nu People never got the credit for building and fertilizing the soil of the State of New York!"

Omari looked at Baraka. "Word up. You talking that cultural Olmec talk, son!"

"We are the rhythm of the heartbeat of this world! If you don't know, learn the real history of Queen Califa of California and the town of Allensworth founded in 1908 by Lt. Colonel, Allensworth, William Payne, Nevada Minor, John A. Palmer, A.M.E. Minister William H. Peck and Henry A. Mitchell."

Jay shook his head and said to Omari, "Mo, I hear what you sayin', but these corporate gangsters are swallowing each block through gentrification without mercy for the poor. They don't care how long our families live here in the city. I have my wifey and three children to think about. That's why I am looking for a way out of here that is a safe place for my children to grow up."

Omari looked at Jay and said, "Black man, I respect your decision for your family, but like the big homie, Nipsey Hussle, from Compton said, 'I just believe in ownership. I believe in investing in yourself. Your foundation should be strong.' I am saving and investing my money now to own a brownstone in the next five years. You have to always believe in the power of yourself, I am going to quote big homie, Nipsey Hussle, again, 'It sounds simple, telling people to work hard and never quit, but to really execute and demonstrate those principles takes discipline and faith.' Those are the two factors that I believe separate the good from the great; the success from failure."

Jay shook his head and said out loud to ensure that his voice was heard. "R.I.P. to the big homie, Nipsey Hussle. I agree we must never forget our connection to our ancestors' historical history to our Afrikan-Paleo ancestors that built triangular-shaped pyramids in the Mississippi Valley around 1500 B.C. that are hidden and distorted by white supremacists to make the world believe we didn't arrive in the Americas until Europeans brought Nu People to North America in slave ships."

Baraka looked at Jay with respect and said to him, "Much respect to all our ancient brothers and siters that carry Kemetic souls in California and throughout the West Coast! Brothers, don't forget Reno, Nevada, was discovered by Nu People."

"We are original thirteenth stars of the United States of America. All fifty states plus the District of Columbia."

With anger in his voice, Jay said, "White supremacists know they been behind, playing catch up with us. That's why they keep enslaving Nu People, by lynching, shooting and contently placing Nu People under biological chemical warfare. We have to keep fighting for our physical and spiritual liberation from the new world government. This entire country belongs to Nu People. Facts!"

Erik looked at his watch. "Yo, sons, Nu People still waiting for reparations around the world for our ancestors' enslavement and unsigned death certifications as being classified as second-class citizens!"

Baraka hung out with his comrades for a while before deciding to take pictures around the community. He began his journey by moving his left leg first, symbolizing his triumph over the demonic spirits of his enemies. He continued walking with his right leg in rhythm with his left, heading down East 115th Street. His camera lens was focused on a police officer who was forcefully pushing a nine-year-old Nu (Black) boy to the ground, falsely attempting to arrest him for shoplifting at a corner store. More police officers quickly arrived, surrounding the young boy.

As Baraka observed this scene, anger welled up inside him. He couldn't help but think of the countless times he had been handcuffed falsely, accused of crimes he didn't commit, which had left painful scars on his wrists. He rubbed his wrists with the palms of his hands, tracing the lingering agony of the affliction. The memory of the fifteen times police had ambushed and assaulted him in his former apartment while he slept in his bed in the middle of the night haunted him.

Baraka reminisced about the nightmare of the last time he was arrested, thinking to himself about the immense pain he had endured every time he tried to get up. He had been kicked repeatedly in the groin and head until he lost consciousness. When he finally awoke, he was completely naked, laying on a cold cement prison cell floor. A correctional officer glared at him with a stern expression, ordering Baraka to get up immediately.

As he struggled to his feet, he was informed that he and Omari would be going to court to determine whether he would stand trial for murder. Baraka stood motionless, his body aching from several bruises all over, looking around in disbelief. His mind then returned to the present, where he listened to the Nu boy's cries for help from his Kemet Nu family.

Baraka took a deep breath as he stood on the block, locked into the pain of his past nightmares and the harsh reality the young brother was enduring due to the traumatization caused by the police officers.

Baraka ran to the corner store, yelling at the officers, "Let the Nu (Black) boy go now!"

The cops drew their guns, threatening to shoot Baraka if he didn't get on his knees immediately.

Baraka yelled back at them, "My freedom and liberation will never allow me to give you the right to lock away the blueprint of my ancestral life!" He refused to succumb to his spirit's call to never become a slave to oppression. Baraka was determined to stay until the young brother was liberated and freed from police custody.

People from the community began to gather around Baraka, demanding the immediate freedom and sovereignty of the young Nu (Black) brother. The police officers looked around, seeing more and more people gathering on the block, their fists clenched, some even carrying guns and knives for protection. The Nu (Black) people were ready to defend the young brother's life with their own, all in the pursuit of spiritual freedom and the right to live as Nu (Black) individuals.

The police officers feared there would be a rebellion if they continued to harm the young brother.

The police officers addressed the crowd gathered in the street, explaining the reason they had stopped the young Nu (Black) brother was because he was wearing colors associated with a street gang.

Baraka was aware that the police were merely using the colors of the young brother's clothing as an excuse to harass him, likely due to the perceived threat posed by the young brother's rich golden-brown skin tone.

Realizing their mistake, the police officers swiftly removed the shackles from the young brother.

People in the crowd raised their Black power fists high, reaching for the sky, paying tribute to the spirits of revolutionary warriors like Afeni Shakur, Zayd Malik Shakur, Lumumba Abdul Shakur, and Mwina Imiri "Sonny Carson." They chanted in unison:

"Brick by brick, wall by wall, we live in the spiritual spirit of all our revolutionaries!"

"Who streets?"

"Our streets!"

"Who streets?"

"Our streets!"

"Brick by brick, wall by wall,

These are our streets!"

The young brother rose to his feet and sprinted toward Baraka, embracing him with tears in his eyes. He thanked everyone in the crowd for saving his life before dashing home to share what had happened to him with his parents.

Baraka looked down at his wrists, refusing to let tears fall, and told himself, "These scars run deep into my soul, where my ancestors speak to my heart in the darkness of the night."

He walked back home, feeling his spirit reenergized, and opened his front door, thinking about how much he loves Lyah. Entering his master bathroom, he turned on a hot shower. As the water cascaded over him, he washed away the blood from his chest, a reminder of the moment the young brother had hugged him.

Chapter Ten

Can a Purple Rose Live in a Jail Cell of
Its Own Pain?

Lyah remained in her private designer fashion room, working throughout the night, seaming a designer dress, stitching lines into the dress to contumely make the fabric come together.

At 1:11 a.m., Lyah unlocked the door and opened the window, inviting the benevolent spirits of her ancestors to fill the room as the spirit of creativity coursed through her soul. She eventually drifted off to sleep on the floor at 5:48 a.m. Lyah's eyes fluttered open at 9:12 a.m., sensing Ra's embrace on her Ka (soul) as the sky welcomed the rain.

Upon waking, Lyah turned around and spotted Baraka seated on the floor in a corner on the right side of the room, gazing at her.

Seeing the rain drops falling on the windowpane, Lyah looked at her husband. "Baraka, we are water people. Wherever land is surround around water Nu people live procreating life through our spiritual birth through our Ancestral connection to water surround around the world!"

Baraka suddenly began to smile as he looked at Lyah, amazed by her brilliance. "Grand Rising my, gorgeous queen Lyah. I always enjoy watching you sleep. Lyah, you are my wife. I do meri (love) you. I will always meri you forevermore in my spirit, but I cannot fight all your insecurities while I am dealing with my own fears in my Jb (heart) to be left alone to face this meri all alone once again by myself without you. If you want this meri (love) to continue on, you have to start trusting me again."

"Grand Rising, my warrior king Baraka," Lyah began, her tone both strong and heartfelt. "You refer to what we're supposed to share as 'This love,' as if it's some object rather than empowering our Meri. Baraka, I won't beg you to stay with me. This is who I am. You can accept me as I am or choose to exit through the front door or the back. But I promise you, if you walk through either door, I will never allow you back into my Jb (heart) again."

Baraka responded, "We've tried going our separate ways before and quickly realized that our Meri grows stronger when we're together, not apart. Lyah, I love you immensely, and forever isn't long enough for me to express it. When we were apart, I missed you every day, deep within my Ka (soul). I can't bear to be separated from you again because you're always on my mind."

Lyah challenged him, saying, "You say that now, but the last time we separated, it was easy for you to walk away."

Baraka sighed and implored, "Why do you keep fighting me, woman? When all I want is to love you? Why? Forget all of that, just come over here so I can kiss your sexy lips!"

Lyah looked away. "I won't simply allow you to treat my Jb (heart) the way you treat the front door. When I opened my Jb (heart) to you, I promised you infinity and gave you a key to unlock my Jb (heart). But when you hurt me by running in and out of the front door, it makes me feel like my Ka (soul) means nothing more to you than a revolving door, something you come in and out of whenever you need my love. And listening to you telling me, 'I will never leave you because you are the only woman I truly love,' doesn't erase the pain you've caused."

"Lyah, our love will always mean the same to me," Baraka stated.

"Not to me, especially when you're hurting me," Lyah replied.

Baraka sighed; frustration evident in his voice. "Lyah, you're overthinking things. Just relax and have faith in us."

"The last time we separated, do you think it was easy for me? Every day, I missed you more."

Baraka looked around the room in amazement at how elegant and unique Lyah's fashion designs were, extraordinary and beautiful. Lyah smiled, gazing at Ra (sun), its magnificent and magical power to heal the soul of all creation. She started dancing, gracefully lifting her legs in the air, laughing as she blew kisses to Baraka. She asked him to dance with her, and he stood to his feet, dancing with her for hours, savoring each other's embrace and affectionate attentiveness.

Lyah said to him, "I've always meri (love) dancing. My parents would take me to the Dance Theatre of Harlem on 446 West 152nd Street to expand my curiosity."

"Who were your sheroes growing up?"

"I had a lot sheroes growing up. My first shero was my mother, Mrs. Kemba Bey. To this day she is my greatest inspiration. She noticed I had an artistry talent when I was a little girl growing up. She understood my originality; how I always chose the uniqueness of fabric designs to broaden my creativity. She taught me how to always be patient with the fabric when designing clothes. My mother is a classically trained seamstress. She told me, 'If you want to become great in your craft, you have to study and have a depth understanding. You will fail and learn to start over again.' She taught me to learn my desired craft to triumph to remain dedicated and determine. My aspiration is to reach the level of success in fashion designing as my second shero, the trailblazer, Zelda Wynn Valdes, to advance fashion designing to a greater inventiveness."

Baraka looked at her with amazement. "Wow, Lyah, your designer dresses, purses, shoes and the rest of your designs are remarkably transformative and beautiful."

"Thank you, Raka. Your masculine scent from your Ka

(soul) feels so great when you hold me! Let me show you more of my designs? The most important thing about fashion designing is to recognize your gifts and talents must be nourished, to create your dream to be a fashion designer. Being a fashion designer takes a lot of hard work, stitching that leads to a consistent of amount of handwork. Fashion drawings takes a lot of effort to remain focus creatively. Shopping for materials takes a lot of time and care. I'm constantly shopping for fabric; high quality fabric is very crucial. I have a unique eye for finding the right fabric and blending colors when I design them into a masterpiece of creation.

"I feel the fabric first against my skin to tap into my creativity and understand how to design each piece. Draping provides me with a glimpse of how the garment will look before I complete it, using muslin fabric on a dress form. After that, it's patternmaking, taking precise measurements, and cutting the fabric accurately. One wrong cut could ruin the entire garment, so sewing the seams correctly is crucial. If it's done incorrectly, it must be redone. I carefully stitch each piece of fabric together until the product meets my exacting standards.

"Before creating a custom-designed garment, I always meet and sit down with every woman to obtain their measurements. I custom-make their dresses to ensure the fabric complements their figure and body type, gaining a better understanding of their preferences. My passion for fashion designing is essential for me to stay motivated and continue growing creatively."

Baraka looked into her eyes. "Lyah, seeing you captivates my Ka (soul). Hearing you express your passion for your craft is inspiring."

Lyah responded warmly, "You have something truly special inside your Ra (soul), too, Baraka."

Baraka smiled as he gazed into Lyah's eyes. "My mind's eye has bestowed blessings through my Spirit, hands, and eyes, allowing me to speak from my consciousness. The gift of developing a collection of photography, canvas painting, and sculpture embodies my Ka (soul)."

Lyah responded affectionately, "I miss staring at your cheeks when you smile, showing your cute cheek dimples."

Baraka chuckled. "Lyah, the Matu Neter, the II laws of God, wrote Law Ausar: 'Your nature is unconquerable peace, therefore nothing in the world can be against you. All experiences come to you to promote your reclamation of peace, that you may, in turn, acquire wisdom and power."

Lyah touched Baraka's cheeks and began to sing his name. "Baraka, Baraka..."

Suddenly, Baraka's cell phone rang, and he glanced at the screen before leaving the room without a word. Ten minutes later, he returned with a smile on his face, arms wide open to hug Lyah. However, she walked away, staring out of the window, refusing to look at him.

Baraka attempted to explain, saying, "Today is a special day. I want to take you somewhere to mark a momentous new beginning in our lives…"

Lyah interrupted. "Was that phone call so special that you had to leave the room to speak to the person in private? I'm trying to share a special moment with you, and you want to keep dwelling in your fears."

"Let me finish, Lyah," Baraka urged.

Lyah countered firmly, "No, Baraka, let me finish. You keep saying I'm the one jeopardizing our Akh (relationship), threatening to leave every time I seek to deepen our love."

Baraka shook his head and took a deep breath before addressing Lyah. "Yo, you keep tripping over nothing."

Lyah questioned, "What did you say?"

Baraka replied, "You heard what I said. It seems all you want to do is argue. I'm not arguing with you anymore."

Lyah retorted, "You are the one tripping. I am not arguing with you."

"We've been arguing for too long, Lyah," Baraka continued. "You treat our home as if it's yours alone, not the home we share together. What's really good, Lyah? I thought we were building something special to one day create a family with our love. Lyah, I am here to stay. I am not going to keep trying to show you how much I love you while you're trying to make me feel like crap. I've never stayed away from home (You) for too long. I'll do anything for your love. I know I act secretive and crazy sometimes, but I am not cheating on you, Lyah…"

Baraka paused for a few seconds to recompose himself before continuing. "I am really a private person sometime. Keeping my emotions deep inside where no one can ever see how deep my pain resides. Lyah, my mind keeps running at night not allowing me to sleep as memories of my past talks to me telling me to keep running away before I get hurt again, but every day and night we are together I know I can rest and sleep knowing our meri truly existence."

Baraka kissed Lyah's hand. "I am faithful to you, but I recognize my actions sometime gives the impression I am cheating to you, for that I sincerely apologizes to you. Lyah, let's stop arguing. A strong Kemet man needs his favorite warrior queen to know how much I need your Jb (heart) to understand how much I need your meri to be my all. Where do we start to fix what is broken in our Akh (relationship)? I need you to—"

Lyah smiled, placing her index finger on his lips. "Start with a kiss and a promise we can share our bed tonight as I lay in your arms, knowing you'll be here when I wake up tomorrow morning."

"I'll promise you only the best of me not just tonight but for the rest of my life."

Baraka twirled Lyah around, now standing behind her, placing his arms around her shoulder, moving his hands, and caressing her hips. Kissing her shoulders softly, he then used the moistness from his tongue to kissing her neck.

Baraka looked into Lyah's eyes, gazing at the sparkle in the center of her brown almond-colored eyes. He winked at her, saying, "The moment I met you, you transformed my life forever. Baby, you are the most fascinating and beautiful woman who has ever captivated my mind…"

Baraka gently took Lyah's hand and guided her into the bathroom, where they prepared a spa experience by running hot water for a steamy bath together. He started undressing her. They both kiss and caressing each other. Baraka marveled at Lyah, staring at every inch of her striking beautiful body. After bathing each other's bodies, they turned the shower on, allowing the water to embrace their bodies as the caressed each other, making sweet tender passionate love for two hours.

Baraka and Lyah fell asleep in each other's arms in the bath. Baraka awakens the next morning at 7:49 a.m., kissing Lyah softly on her back to show her how much he meris kissing her ravishing rich golden brown skin. Lyah slowly opened her eyes from a deep sleep, looking at Barack, blowing a meri kiss to him.

"Grand Rising, Baraka. I know you give more than just kisses and words to me. You give the best of yourself to love all of me."

"Grand Rising to you as well, Lyah. I had a dream about you when I was sleeping last night, visualizing us holding hands and walking on the beach in Coney Island… Lyah listen to me. We are going to get through this. While you were sleeping last night, you were moving around more then you normally do. Did you have a dream last night?"

Lyah couldn't wipe away all the tears in her eyes as she tried to hide her emotions from Baraka. She washed her face with warm water and said, "I relive that day when I was in labor, giving birth to our baby when my holistic doula confirmed what the physician already told me, that our baby Mutulu was born stillborn. I relive that moment in my mind every day."

Baraka kissed Lyah on her forehead and gently said, "Ayo, Lyah, you have to stop dwelling in your pain because if you don't breathe, you're going to drown. I want to save you, but you keep swimming further into the ocean where I can't see you anymore, past your..."

Lyah interrupted Baraka, tears in her eyes, and said to him, "I don't understand your analogy because there is no ocean. I am not swimming or drowning."

Baraka gently wiped away more tears forming in her eyes. "Lyah, your tears are the ocean you are drowning in. I remember the day I walked into Mutulu's room, and you told me you had finished the last part of painting Mutulu's room. I looked around the room and was taken aback by how beautifully you had painted it in red, blue, and white, the divine colors of our ancestors of life. I walked around the room, examining the details of the painting. You tapped me on my shoulder and told me you had another surprise for me, pointing to the ceiling. When I looked up, I was amazed by the spectacular canvas painting of the sky with silver stars on the ceiling. We chose his Ren (name) to be Mutulu Diara Asari-Dokubo. I hear Mutulu's cry echoing in my Ka (soul) when I close my eyes to go to sleep at night sometimes. I hear him laughing every time I pass his bedroom when I am alone in the hallway. You're right, Raka. I know you want to talk about Mutulu, but..."

She started feeling dizzy as she continued to cry. "I cannot talk about it right now."

Baraka held her tightly in his arms as they embraced each other in the bathtub.

He kissed Lyah's smooth, soft, golden, rich brown skin and said, "Gorgeous, stop crying! I've got you for life! You know it hurts me to see you cry. I can't stand it when you cry. I feel so weak, like I'm not protecting you."

Baraka began to wipe her tears from her face as they started sharing silly jokes.

"Lyah, I have a love thang in my Ka (soul) for you. You got me wrapped around your Jb (heart)."

"Baraka, you are doing a lot of finessing this morning. I know I got your Jb." Lyah passionately kissed Baraka's left neck.

"Wow, girl, you got some magic in those lips. Lyah, do you remember our first date?"

Lyah kissed Baraka. Passionately licking her lips, she said, "You are so delicious! Of course, I remember our first date like it was yesterday. I bet you don't remember what I was wearing."

"Most definitely I do! We agreed to meet at 328 Malcolm X Boulevard in front of Sylvia's restaurant. You wore a white midi bodycon dress, showing off your shoulders with a gold ankle bracelet. You amazed my Ka with your beauty."

"You looked so handsome with your three-piece cranberry fitted suit and silk black and cranberry striped tie.'

Baraka bent down, kissing Lyah's inner thigh, saying, "You taste divinely good!"

"You are so nasty. You know how to please me right. I remember I didn't want to be late for our first date. I made reservations at Sylvia's restaurant for 7:30 p.m. I rushed out the house. When I arrived at the restaurant, I stood out front, checking my watch. I will never forget that day as long as I live—you walked up to me with grace. You looked so stunningly beautiful."

"As we entered the restaurant, the waiter seated us in the back and handed us our menus. The food at Sylvia's restaurant was delicious," Baraka reminisced.

"Our second date was at Amy Ruth's restaurant, and you wore a vintage printed midi bodycon dress," he continued. "We had a great time getting to know each other better."

"When I first started courting you, we always had fun," Baraka sighed. "What happened to us, Lyah?"

Lyah responded, "I don't know, Baraka, I really don't. But I agree, we need to get out of this house. I'd love to join you for breakfast at that café you mentioned the other night while you were taking photography pictures of the streets that caught your interest."

They stepped out of their luxurious gold clawfoot tub, using toweling each other dry. Smiles exchanged, and they shared tender kisses before proceeding to get dressed.

Baraka was an incredibly attractive man—his strength and sex appeal were undeniable. A single glance into his enigmatic eyes was enough to make any woman feel weak in the knees. The mere thought of his masculine, powerful physique touching them was simply overwhelming. He moved with a unique sense of quiet power, setting him apart from other men. In front of the mirror, he meticulously attended to his crisp fade haircut, ensuring his waves were perfectly aligned. His dark eyebrows and beard were impeccably groomed. He applied geranium-scented cologne to both sides of his neck, then adorned himself with a gold ankh necklace. Dressing in his custom Dapper Dan sweatsuit adorned with red and black symbols and a reversible leather vintage Dapper Dan jacket, he completed his outfit with retro classic Air Force 1 sneakers. Studying his reflection in the hallway mirror, he flexed, licked his lips, and even winked at himself, empowered by his warrior Kemetic spirit.

Baraka had grabbed his camera bag and walked over to Lyah. He gazed into Lyah's captivating and melodic eyes, admiring her seductive Kemetic Nubian beauty, which seemed kissed by the sun and accentuated by her rich caramel brown skin tone. Lyah was seated on the living room couch, tending to her natural long curls, elegantly draping them over her left shoulder. She carefully adorned her right and left ears with bamboo sterling silver hoop earrings. Applying nude lip-gloss to her lips, she then reached for a bottle of strawberry lotion, moisturizing her hands, legs, and feet with care. Afterward, she slipped on her high heels, prompting Baraka to look at her pocketbook and high heels, about to say something.

"Ayo, what are you doing?"

"I am getting dressed. What are you doing?"

"Lyah, you look so sexy. Did you make the purple silk couture dress you are wearing?"

"Yes, I did Sir. I also made the high heels and the pocketbook I am wearing too."

"Your dress is really beautiful. I am digging your high heel and pocketbook game."

"Thank you, Baraka, for noticing…"

Lyah reached out her left hand, grasping Baraka's right hand to help her stand. She smiled into his eyes and adjusted his jacket collar before closing her eyes and said, "We have to say a prayer before leaving the house. Let's pray to Wepwawet."

"Wepwawet, opener of the way, bless your coming and going. Open the way for Baraka and me, and for those we love. Close the way for those who seek to do us harm. Wepwawet, opener of the way, bless our coming and going from left to right. Hotep Wepwawet."

After their prayer, Baraka unlocked the front door and held Lyah's left hand as they descended the steps of their brownstone. They walked together, chasing the New York wind, listening to the wind's whispers, fully embracing the moment, determined to make it unforgettable. They felt the powerful spirit of the wind clearing obstacles from their path, a connection to their Ka (souls) and the greater world around them.

Chapter Eleven

I Refuse to Walk in Your Tears in the Dark Bare Feet as I Demand for My Complete Liberation

Lyah and Baraka walked down the street, seeing many of their friends as they greeted each of them with meri. Baraka and Lyah continued toward the café, stopping at a stop light before crossing the street. Baraka noticed three men standing outside of the restaurant, smoking cigarettes and talking to each other. As soon as the three men noticed Lyah, they immediately stopped talking. Her incredible beauty had completely captivated them. They then made their way toward her, trying to approach her discreetly, with the aim of taking her away from Baraka. One of the men tried to open the front entrance door of the restaurant for Lyah, giving Baraka a hostile look.

Baraka looked at them in the eyes as he pinched his nose, telling, "Get out of the way now!"

All three of the men clenched their fists, noticing the intensity in Baraka's gaze. One of the men then glanced at

Lyah and blew her a kiss before turning to Baraka and saying, "Word is born, my man, you better hold onto your wisdom (Black woman) tighter than that! When I make my move to take her, I promise you, she's going to be mine, and I won't be giving her back to you! Word!"

The other two men blocked the doorway, refusing to move out of the way, sizing up Baraka.

Baraka stood strong with no fear in his heart, studying the mathematics of each of their stances, visualizing the way he would have to move if they wanted to fight him. Baraka looked at them, saying, "Ayo, back the fuck up, son! Try to move reckless on me, you gonna find out ain't nothing sweet over here!"

The men backed up, nodding as Baraka opened the door for Lyah. He smiled at them, giving them a head nod as he grabbed Lyah by the waist, kissing her passionately on the lips. Lyah smiled into Baraka's eyes as they entered the restaurant.

Lyah looked around the restaurant and said to Baraka, "This restaurant looks really nice."

"Lyah, when are you going to open your own boutique?"

Lyah responded, quoting Madam C.J. Walker, "I had to make my own living and my own opportunity. But I made it! Don't sit down and wait for the opportunity to come. Get up and make them.' I take Madam C.J. Walker's words to heart. I've already purchased a building that I like. I'm in the process of drafting the technical details for the structure to establish the cornerstone of my business. I'm working with an architect to lay the groundwork for the landscape to set my boutique apart from others."

Baraka looked at her. "You never told me you already purchased a building."

"You never asked, and besides, we've been arguing lately. I'm channeling my Black girl magic within me. I can't sit around crying all day." She smiled with her head tilted. "Madam C. J. Walker famously said, 'I got my start by giving myself a start.'"

"I can't wait to see the boutique. I'm ambitiously proud of your audacity to live out your dreams."

"I'm extremely fascinated and enchanted by your sculpture arts of welding, painting, and canvas sketching, and your photographic portraits of the global community. You have thousands of sculptures, sketches, paintings, and pictures. You're ready to open your own art gallery. I'm proud of you, Baraka. I find myself religiously studying your structural, textural, and unique artwork forms."

Baraka and Lyah sat down at a table in the café as Lyah heard her favorite singer, Aaliyah's, song "I Don't Wanna." Placing her hands over her face, looking at Baraka, they both laugh. They sat next to a window. Lyah stared up at the sky, looking at the full moon change colors from sapphire blue to violet purple before eclipsing in the sky.

The waitress walked up to their table, giving them the breakfast menus, introducing herself, and smiling as she stared at Baraka's physical physique. "Good morning, my name is

Tonya. I will be your waitress. You all look so cute together. How can I help both of you on this beautiful morning?"

Lyah looked at the menu. "I am thinking about having strawberry pancakes, honey beef sausages, and orange juice. But I don't know what I want yet. Baraka, what are you going to order?"

Tonya cut her eyes at Lyah as she stared at Baraka's structure-built body, staring him up and down, smiling at him.

Baraka wasn't paying attention to Tonya; he focused the energy of his Ka (soul) on his universal queen Lyah. He blew a kiss at Lyah. "Baby boo. I am hungry, those strawberry pancakes sound good. You going to have to share some of those pancakes with me."

"Baraka, if you are hungry, why don't you just order some strawberry pancakes for yourself?"

"I am hungry for you, Lyah."

"Baraka, since you are so handsome. I might share one strawberry pancake with you, if you act right!"

Baraka, leaned over the table and kissed Lyah's neck and lips softly, whispering into her ear. "You know that one strawberry pancake is not enough to satisfy me. You know it will never taste like you so it will never satisfy my desires!" He sat back in his seat, staring at Lyah's sexy thighs. He winked at her, smiling as he licked his lips, showing his deep cheek dimples. With his deep, baritone voice, he said, "I am considering sausages and cheese omelet with an avocado on the side."

Tonya looked at Lyah and said, "That's cute, seeing you with your boo."

"Yeah, he's my boo, but he's also my husb—"

Tonya interrupted Lyah, dismissing her presence. "If you are not ready to order, I'll come back when you are ready. Don't hesitate to let me know when you are ready to order." Tonya turned her back to Lyah, swinging her thick thighs, moving closer to Baraka, rubbing her hip against his broad left shoulder.

He moved away from Tonya, raising his hands. "Yo, chill. I am with my queen!"

Tonya was determined to have Baraka for herself, and she wouldn't accept "no" as an answer. She seductively licked her lips and said to Baraka, "I want you to look through the menu really carefully to find a cuisine that satisfies you. If you don't find anything on the menu that you desire, I know if you come back for the dinner cuisine later tonight, sweetie, I'll make sure there will be enough favors on the menu to strengthen your desires to come back for more."

Lyah jumped to her feet. "Fake bitches always want to eat off the floor, trying to take another woman's husband. Ms. Savage, you ain't woman enough to take my man. Little girl, keep it moving, with your desperate attempt to steal my man!"

"Girl, please, look at my body." Tonya bent over, sticking out her butt and breast. "I don't have to try. If I want to, I'll just take your man right now in front of you!"

"You are so pitiful, Ms. Savage, it's bad enough you look ratchet, you want to act ratchet, too. Girl, bye. You are too pitiful."

"I already told you my name is Tonya. My name is not Ms. Savage."

"Girl, bye. I don't care what your name is." Lyah pointed in Tonya's face. "Bye, girl. You're not even a competition to me. Look at me and look at you? You cannot compare the uniqueness of the mysteriousness of my remarkable beauty to your bumpy repulsive face. Little mama, I guess I shouldn't blame you for being so jealous of me and my Akh (relationship). Bye, girl. I am not going to keep wasting my time talking to you. You're not worth my time. You are trash. So, keep eating off the floor, Ms. Savage. You wish you were me."

"Girl, nobody thinking about you. I don't want to be you."

Lyah crossed her legs with cultivation with a feminine refine sophistication, and raised her left hand, showing Tonya her diamond wedding ring saying to Tonya, "Yes, you do."

People sitting at tables in the restaurant start pointing at Tonya, laughing at her.

Two Haitian-Dominican sisters named Esther and Henrietta Dessalines-Garrido, who were from the province of Pedernales in the Dominican Republic, moved to the Bronx when they were thirteen and eleven years old with their parents, Jacques and Clair Dessalines-Garrido.

Jacques and Clair Dessalines-Garrido were forced to leave their beloved home of Pedernales, Dominican Republic on July 19, 2014, with Esther, Henrietta, and their youngest daughter,

Vivian Dessalines-Garrido, with only the clothes they were wearing to avoid murderous execution by government assailants because of the Dessalines-Garrido family's ethnic heritage of Haitian and Dominican descent and their highly melanin skin tone. The government questioned the Dessalines-Garrido family's citizenship in the Dominican Republic.

Both Jacques and Clair Dessalines-Garrido were born in Pedernales, as were their parents. They tried to prove their loyalty and citizenship to the Dominican Republic but faced hopelessness and fear of the future living there without birth certification. Jacques, Clair, and their children were considered Haitian by the Dominican Republic government because they didn't have birth certificates to prove they were official citizens of the Dominican Republic.

Jacques led his family in the darkest of nights on a secret small boat that was transporting native Haitians and Haitian Dominicans to Miami, Florida. When they arrived in Miami a day and a half after leaving the Dominican Republic, Clair Dessalines-Garrido called her second cousin, Marie Santos-Montou, who lives in the Southwest Bronx. Marie Santos-Montou wired Clair one hundred and fifty-five dollars to survive until she arrived in Miami in two days. When Marie Santos-Montou and her husband, Alberto Vasquez-Montou Sr., drove for twenty hours, taking three rest breaks before arriving in Miami, Florida. When they arrived, they began hugging and kissing Clair, Jacques, Esther, Henrietta, and Vivian. They were overwhelmed with excitement as they all drove to the Southwest Bronx, New York City, to Marie and Alberto Sr.'s home, which they shared with their seven children: Alberto Jr., Janet, Hector, Alvin, Sergio, Tifany, and Alexandrea.

A day after they arrived home, Maria went to a party store and grocery store buying items to celebrate her family's arrival in America. She surprised her cousins by giving them a party to ensure they felt safe and happy in their new home. Jacques and Clair Dessaline-Garrido were concerned because they didn't speak English, and they wouldn't be able to financially provide for their children. Alberto Sr. said to them in Spanish, 'Te ayudaré hasta que puedas mantener a tus hijos' (I will help until you are able to provide for your children). He helped them to gain temporary visas and political asylum to stay in the United States of America. Alberto Sr. assisted Jacques and Clair in finding employment at a hotel in Queens, New York City within the housekeeping department.

Jacques and Clair dedicated their time and commitment to providing their daughters with a better life in America. Eighteen months later, they were able to get their own two-bedroom apartment in the Bronx. The Dessaline-Garrido family missed the Dominican Republic with all of their hearts, but in due time, they learned to adjust to their new environment in the United States of America. The Bronx became the Dessaline-Garrido family's second home.

Esther an Henrietta were sitting at a table in a restaurant across from Lyah and Baraka. Esther and Henrietta said in unison, "Mama, you are doing way too much. You are so ratchet and pitiful for thinking you could take that woman's husband. Pick up your face off the floor and hurry up and walk away before someone steps on your face!"Baraka looked at Lyah. "Wow… You know I am yours forevermore! Let's go to a different restaurant."

"You are right. I don't trust her to serve me my food. I don't know what she would put in my food before she serves it to me. Where do you want to go now Baraka to eat? Because I am hungry!"

"I know this Poetry café that's lit on 142nd Street that services African American soul food and Kemetic-Nubian cuisines with spices and blend tastes with red velvet pancakes baked berry Dama Be Potaatas, kofta and baseema breakfast."

"What is the poetry cafe name?"

"Translated in English it's called Taste of Neteru (God) Food in Your Soul. The food is more expensive but it's worth it. They serve Harlem's famous chicken and waffles. When you taste the food, you'll love the food, desiring more."

Baraka stood to his feet and extended his right hand for Lyah to take. Lyah smiled at Baraka and reached out with her left hand. Just before he could grasp her hand, she playfully moved it away. Baraka then bent down on one knee, gazing into her eyes, and gently caressed both of her hands. He softly kissed her knees and spoke with authority.

"Fear not."

"What?"

"I am a strong Kemet (Black) man. Fear not the original man is here!"

Lyah stumbled, feeling hot and began laughing. "I cannot take you anywhere. Don't you ever forget I am a queen goddess, Mother Creator and Father Creator original daughter!"

"I cannot help myself, Lyah. I lose all control when I am around you. Your meri brings me to the peak of culmination within my Ka (soul). True intimacy is want I desire from our Akh (relationship). Meri is not enough."

Lyah rubbed the top of Baraka's head, softly kissing both sides of Baraka's neck.

Chapter Twelve

When Will You Forgive Yourself/Me to
Meri (Love) Again?

Lyah and Baraka walked out of the restaurant, hand in hand, strolling along the sidewalk for eighteen blocks. They eventually arrived at the street where Taste of Neteru Café was situated. Baraka pointed across the street to the café's sign and said to Lyah.

"Lyah, we have to cross the street now. Taste of Neteru Café is across the street."

Baraka and Lyah stood patiently on the sidewalk, observing several cars driving past them on the bustling street. Once all the cars had cleared the street, they crossed over and entered Taste of Neteru Café. Upon opening the front door, they immediately noticed that a poetry jam was getting underway inside the cafe.

Lyah glanced around, absorbing the serene ambiance of Taste of Neteru Café, while Afro beats played in the background by the deejay. She enjoyed the sounds of conscious-minded individuals engaging in conversations and sharing laughter.

Baraka took out his camera and began capturing moments of the Nubian family peacefully gathering together, snapping pictures of the scene.

As Lyah and Baraka walked by, they noticed a man wearing a red t-shirt featuring a portrait from January 17, 1972. The image depicted members of the Black Panther Party, Erika Huggins and Afeni Shakur, holding hands in a gesture of unity during a Black Panther Party rally in Los Angeles, California. This event celebrated the lives of the Black Panther Party Southern Los Angeles leader Alprentice "Bunchy" Carter and Erika Huggins' husband, John Huggins, both of whom were prominent members of the Black Panther Party. Tragically, Bunchy Carter and John Huggins were assassinated on January 17, 1969, on the campus of the University of California, Los Angeles.

The t-shirt displayed Erika Huggins and Afeni Shakur standing side by side, raising their right fists to the heavens on the front. On the back of the shirt, there was a portrait of Erika Huggins' eldest daughter, Mai Huggins, and Afeni Shakur's two adult children, Tupac Shakur and Sekyiwa Shakur. This image commemorated an April 6, 1993 protest march in West Oakland, California, marking the twenty-fifth anniversary of the assassination of the first Black Panther Party member, Robert James "Lil Bobby" Hutton, which occurred on April 6, 1968. During the protest, Mai Huggins and Afeni Shakur's children raised their fists to the heavens in remembrance.

Baraka looks at the artistry of the t-shirt as he approaches the brother extended his right hand saying to him 'Hotep King, I am an artist. I am digging the powerful meaning of your t-shirt.'

Baraka examined the artwork on the t-shirt as he approached the brother. He then extended his right hand and said to him, "Yo god, what time is it?"

"Hotep, king. It's Nation Time!"

"Peace, king, peace!'

The man then looked at Lyah and said, "Hotep, beautiful queen. Hotep, king. My name is Yashan Olugbala. I am a graphic designer."

Baraka squeezed his own nose, nodding his head and smiling at Yashan as he said, "Yashan Olugbala, I can look into your eyes and see you are carrying history in your Ka (soul). Warrior Yashan Olugbala, where are you from?"

Yashan responded, "Ungawa, brother. I grew up in both Atlantic City, New Jersey, and Brick City (Newark, New Jersey), the birthplace of Atlantic City, New Jersey Revolutionary Liberator Lumumba Abdul Shakur. I grew up listening to my grandparents' old Chris Columbo jazz records; I would listen to them all the time. When I was between the ages of five to ten years old, I would run around the business district of downtown on Kentucky Avenue, chilling on the curb and chasing the fine girls in Atlantic City. When I was ten years old, my parents moved my two sisters and me to 'Brick City' Newark, New Jersey. That's when I learned more about the great people born in Newark, like social justice great leader Amiri Baraka, scholar Dr. Leonard Jefferies, Marvelous Marvin Hagler, the late great silky alluring elegance of jazz musician queen Sarah Vaughan, and the great sophisticated brilliant queen Whitney Houston. In Brick City, we rise above the fire to fight for our freedom!"

Baraka responded, "Word up. Big ups to New Jersey! Warrior Yashan, I am captivated by the graphic design of the front and the back of your t-shirt!"

Baraka presented Yashan with his art portfolio, showcasing his graphic and painting designs. Each of Baraka's artistic illustrations portrayed a border sphere from an Afrocentric perspective. Yashan scrutinized the eloquent creativity evident in Baraka's artistic compositions, which featured sketches and photographic images.

As they examined the artwork, Baraka and Yashan engaged in a conversation about potential future collaborations.

Yashan turned to Baraka and said, "I have seen some of your work throughout my travels. Baraka, here's my business card, we should continue our connection to build to create ideas together for a business venture." Yashan turned around to see four of his homies at a table, yelling for him to come over. With an excited smile on his face, he raised his hands in the air and loudly said in his friend's direction, "Whut up doe? I see my people waving to me in the back of the café to join them at a table. Let me introduce you and your queen to my homies before you go to your table."

Yashan walked up to his homies, who were sitting in the back, engaged in a heated argument about classic hip-hop and the modern era of drill and trap music. He introduced Baraka and Lyah to his friends. They all greeted Baraka and Lyah with a head nod and a Black power fist.

Coltrane, one of Yashan's friends, turned his attention to them. "How are you living, Black man? Nubian sister, peace and blessings to you!"

Lyah responded with a friendly smile. "Peace, peace!"

Coltrane then looked at Baraka and Lyah and asked, "What's the supreme mathematics born today?"

Baraka and Lyah replied in unison, "Culture freedom is reborn today!"

Coltrane nodded in acknowledgment and said, "Peace. Knowledge is born!"

Baraka smiled at Coltrane and said, "We were living righteously, king."

Coltrane nodded, then balled up his right and left fists together, placing them in front of his chest as a gesture of respect toward Baraka and Lyah.

Another of Yashan's friends, Tevin, spoke confidently to Baraka, saying, "Peace, warrior king! Much respect and honor to you, queen!"

Tevin continued his conversation with another homie named Cory, who was sitting at the table with him. He said, "Yo, Cory, you were really starting to feel yourself with that battery pack on your back, but you will always be little bro (brother) to me."

Cory responded, "Pause, it ain't my fault, homie, that old school hip-hop is losing in the game. You have to accept that drill and trap music is winning. Don't get mad at me, Tevin, that you kept dropping your books, and now I am the teacher of the new school!"

Another friend, Mo, chimed in. "Yo, Mo, pause, pull down your skirt. I only speak real hip-hop when I spit facts, when I speak of our native tongue of culture of hip-hop."

Corey replied, "Tevin, I respect what you're saying. hip-hop is life to my soul, but—"

Tevin interrupted. "But nothing. Ayo, my dude, I am starting to see your panties!"

Cory adjusted his vintage brim cap embroidered with the letters "NYC," then stood up, facing Tevin with anger in his eyes. He bit down on his bottom lip, staring at Tevin.

Tevin, in response, also stood up and said to Cory, "You already know who I am. What do you want to do?"

Yashan stood between Cory and Tevin. "Ayo, warrior kings, we need to pause this. I thought we were building a mathematic cypher of Black brotherhood of knowledge."

Cory turned to Tevin and looked at him. "Ayo, son, your mouth is starting to get real greasy. Watch your mouth when you speak to me! I love hip-hop, too, but if someone is not moving with money in hip-hop, they are only stuttering speaking to me. I don't speak a broken language like it doesn't speak money converted into change. If hip-hop doesn't make me money, I don't have a need for it in my life. I'm like a transformer, always moving and changing, adapting to every move in the game. That's why I've been a natural-born hustler since I came out of my mother's womb, facts! Hip-hop runs deep in my veins, beating into my heart. There are murals painted on blocks and walls throughout my borough, depicting the iconic history of the early foundations of hip-hop. That's why I always rep my borough to the fullest. I go hard every day, building up these blocks, putting my blood and sweat into these streets. I am a native New Yorker!"

Baraka glanced around the restaurant as a waitress approached Lyah and Baraka, informing them that she had found a nice table for them. Baraka then turned to look at Yashan and his friends. "Peace, warrior kings. We'll build later, my queen and I are going to head to our table before someone else takes the table."

Baraka and Lyah moved around the restaurant, spotting an empty table next to a window where the sun was shining through. They sat down at the table, basking in the warmth of the sun on a beautiful day. Lyah rested her elbow on the table, placing her left hand under her chin, and gazed deeply into Baraka's eyes. He licked his lips.

She looked at him. "Your sexiness is seductive to my spirit!"

"Lyah, you saved me. I remember the first time I saw you, Lyah, I was chilling on the block with Omari, Jay, Erik and the rest of my homies. Omari and I just came home from serving time in the federal penitentiary. I couldn't look away as I stared at you, you were with that lame sucker Derek. He brought you around the block as if you were his trophy. All the homies on the block start hawking as they all stared at you because they wanted you but, they were too afraid of Derek to think about taking you from him. I knew you were my purpose from that moment since the first time I saw you. I stood in my revolutionary stance, giving Derek a head nod. Derek walked up to me with his trunk ice black diamond jewelry holding your left hand, Derek introduced you to me. Feeling he cannot be touched because his fam (family) are notorious street savages.

"His cockiness made him vulnerable to my ambition to take you from him. Derek thought no one can take you from him because his fam (family) murder game was tight. That when I knew he fuck up, not recognizing the weight my name carries in the streets. I took off my stunner shades smiling into your gorgeous almond rich brown eyes. When I stared into your eyes, I licked my lips telling myself "Fuck Derek and his street family, I am going take you from him. I repeatedly told myself, I am going to make you mine!" Watching you walk away with him, I strategy my next move.

"Hit a lick moving up the game, telling myself every time I saw you, I was going to take you from Derek. I shot my shot to get with you, knowing you were meant for me. I worked my charm on you for two months to convince you to be mine.

When we started dating, I was so amazed by your intellectual beauty, you are philosophic vastly versatile. You challenge me in ways my Spirit carved to deepen my understanding. A month after taking you from Derek, I bum rushed the front door of his house sticking up his bitch ass for his ghetto green and trunk ice jewelry. I really am in love with you, Lyah. I've changed in so many ways that I will never go back to the block. Consciousness has a purpose in my life that my past endures can never replace. I am dedicated to saving lives by building up our community."

Lyah stared at him. "There is a war raging against our Afrikan Nation around the world that many of our people are refusing to stop fighting one another to strategize to fight against a nefarious oppressive global system of white supremacy."

Baraka nodded in agreeance. "Words not spoken in life has a consequence when death comes. Within seconds, life can quickly change. Six years ago, my big homey D-Train was murdered, saving his ten-year-old daughter, Tami, who was walking home from school when she was sexually harassed in her apartment building hallway by four undercover cops. After D-Train, picked up his fraternal twin son and daughter, Haki and Khadijah, from pre-school. D-Train walked into his apartment building hallway. He noticed four undercover cops in the hallway standing next to Tami. When D-Train approached them, one of the undercover cops pulled out his gun, pointing it at Tami. D-Train feared for his daughter's life; he wrestled with the cop as the other undercover cops shot him in his head and back. D-Train died a horrific death on the cold cemented floor as his children, Tami, Haki and Khadijah witnessed his murder.

"Back in the day, when I struggled to stop hustling on the block, I would go back to my apartment to go to sleep. I would close my eyes and couldn't sleep from hearing D-Train's voice echo in my ka, telling me I was trapped in-between two worlds in the streets, serving two different masters. I knew I had to finally change my life. A lot in my life has changed in the past six years since I've been studying my lessons to improve my life. I, sometimes, hang on the block with my big homies and young homies, standing on my square, to create a cipher to dispel white supremacy, speaking Ma'at to unlock the Kemetic wisdom of our ancestors. The law of Ma'at, is written. God needs you in order to come into the world. Fulfilling God's need is the highest act of love, and only through your love for God, you can fulfill your love of God in the world for the protection of the world."

Lyah listened to him carefully and then said, "To quote Neely Fuller Jr., 'If you do not understand white supremacy, what it is, and how it works, everything else that you understand will only confuse you."

Baraka looked at her. "Your Ka (soul) is phenomenal."

"What did you say, Baraka?"

"I have embraced the Law of Sekher in my Ka. Law of Sekher is 'When the emotions of a man manifest in response to the world of God, they have the power to influence the course of any and all events in the world." Baraka smiled at her. "The most beautiful Lyah, your Ka is phenomenal. I never thought meri will ever happen to me." Baraka reached across the table, caressing Lyah's soft, tender hands. "I lost my way while trying to find my way to you, Lyah. There was a time when I succumbed to my frustration, my hurt, and my fears. But ever since I met you, I no longer focus on my fears; I reach out to a higher power, Mother Creator and Father Creator. I've chosen not to cling to the pain of my past, reminding myself that this isn't the end. I must follow my Spirit. Lyah, a part of me wants to keep running, but my heart is weary of running. I find myself on unfamiliar street corners, trying not to think about you, but then I catch your sweet scent in the wind and hear your voice in my soul."

"I fell asleep two nights ago while listening to Jazmine Sullivan's album *Heaux Tales*, dreaming about you, Baraka. I won't apologize for wondering whether you think about me enough. Sometimes, you scare me when you walk out the door without telling me if or when you'll return home to me."

"I will never leave you, never. I use my camera to communicate through my soul, awakening the masses of Kemet Nu to our greatness as the original warriors of the universe. I am fearless in my audacity, soaring with the spirit of a falcon. I carry my cameras with me everywhere because art is my therapy. My spirit chose for me to come into this lifetime when my parents united their spiritual strength, ensuring that

I could overcome anything. I am grateful to my parents for instilling in my veins the freedom of all our ancestors who dared to dream audaciously of liberation, especially when my mother conceived me."

Baraka and Lyah leaned in to kiss each other, uncertain of how to escape the pain of their past but aware that their union was divinely golden, destined to bless their future, and create a cycle of blessings repeatedly. They kissed, cherishing the moment, hoping it would forever reside in their Ka (souls), as the seconds stood still in their hearts (Jb).

A man named Zion El-Keif and four of his friends—Khalid Shabazz, Jah, Khaseekhemwy, and Perneb—walked into the poetry café with confidence in their Ka (souls), seeking breakfast and a chance to enjoy the vibrant poetry. Zion and three of his friends had all grown up in the Bronxdale Housing Projects in the Bronx, New York City. Khalid Shabazz was from East London, England, with family roots dating back to the fourth century A.D. He had arrived in America three years ago at the age of twenty-one, along with his parents and younger sister, Kembe.

"I always protect my Creator and my ancestors, speaking facts about hip-hop culture. Grandmaster Flowers from "BK" Brooklyn was one the pioneers of hip-hop pioneers of hip-hop culture in Brooklyn, that cultivated the ones and twos of the records turntables. Grandmaster Flowers mixing of funk and instrumental into the art of hip-hop streets beats. Many people from Bronxdale Housing Projects don't get their respect for helping pioneering party beats in the parks and streets. We lost a lot of icon pioneers of hip-hop culture from Bronxdale Housing Projects since 1971."

Jah smiled. "Mo, it's funny that you say that. My uncle Tee would tell me stories about when he was growing up in the Bronxdale Housing Project. He would tell me Rosedale Avenue was always jamming with parties in the summertime. He told me him and his homeboys would go all around the Bronx, Manhattan, and Brooklyn breakin' and winning local competitions in the streets, moving the crowd at block parties. He told me he used to see Deejay Kool Herc all the time walking or driving from Bronx River to the Soundview section of the Bronxdale Housing Projects to learn from Kool DJ Dee and Disco King Mario how to cultivate the energy in the crowd with magnetic power of soul music."

Zion smiled. "I honor Deejay Cool Herc for him advancing the structure of the breakbeats with his version of the crossfading, Deejay Cool Herc help B-boy breaking extended the beat to allow the breakers to move better with mixing the beat. Yo, we must never forget Emcee Coke LA Rock back in the day. If you saw Cool Herc deejaying at a party, you would see Coke LA Rock rocking Deejay Cool Herc parties."

"I respect and will always play homage to both Deejay Cool Herc and Emcee Coke LA Rock for their historical and legendary dedication to the culture of hip-hop. I most definitely respect Deejay Cool Herc as a pioneer with the culture of hip-hop. I just want the historical truth of hip-hop cultural to be written factual without lies. My father would tell me the history of the early pioneers in hip-hop in the Bronxdale Housing Projects. Telling me stories about how the culture was formed by the innovations from the icon unsung heroes of hip-hop culture by the likes of Kool DJ Dee, Pete DJ Jones, Tyrone The Mixologist, Sinbad, Grand Wizard Theodore, Disco Twins, Disco King Mario, and other great hip-hop pioneers throughout New York City. My big homies told me Disco King Mario and Kool DJ Dee helped build a foundation for hip-hop that they never received their hip-hop flowers for helping to create the hip-hop culture."

Zion stretched out his arms, waving to a waitress to get her attention so he could order his food.

Perneb licked his lips with a serious look on his face. "I was watching Michael Wayne's documentaries the other day about the early days of hip-hop culture. The more I learn about the culture of hip-hop I am amazed. Yo, some people timeline being founders of hip-hop." Perneb paused to gather his words, looking down, shaking his head.

Zion said to Perneb, "Black man, what are you saying?"

He then looked at Zion. "Yo, son, do the math? Some people that said they were a part of the hip-hop culture lied by manipulating the truth. The original pioneers of hip-hop culture can never be erased from building the groundwork to create hip-hop culture. Many people date, time and places of their history to the culture is built around lies and manipulation of deception. The real pioneers of hip-hop culture is written in the moon where the universal history will know forever who the originators of hip-hop culture really are."

Zion said, "Mo, I have much respect for 1520 Sedgwick Avenue, but we must understand the elements of hip-hop culture reach beyond the Bronx River Housing Project. But I do honor and respect the imprint of hip-hop that was created in Bronx River Housing Projects, advancing hip-hop culture beyond the project buildings. The people of hip-hop culture owe the pioneers of Bronx River Housing Projects a lot of respect."

Jah rubbed his hands together. "Facts, true indeed, but I'm tired of people erasing Kool DJ Dee and Disco King Mario from the early foundation of hip-hop culture. If you watch Michael Wayne's documentaries, you'll find numerous hip-hop pioneers who acknowledge the influences of Kool DJ Dee, Disco King Mario, and other pioneers on the careers of many hip-hop legends. People who knew Disco King Mario often reminisce about how he could unite crowds from different neighborhoods, playing break beats that brought Bronxdale Boys (B-Boys) together to breakdance to the rhythm. During Disco King Mario's park shows, the Black Spades gang would always be present, wearing their jackets. The Black Spades were heavily influenced by the Black consciousness movement of the 1960s and early 1970s, and they brought vitality to the streets to combat any oppression with force. They were notorious for defeating their enemies using body armor and weapons. Disco King Mario was trained in combat as a Black Spade, and every time he DJed, he moved the crowd. The crowd would go wild, watching Disco King Mario perform his signature snake dance move, exciting all the girls in the crowd."

Jah nodded. "Mo, I heard from my family members how they would see Grandmaster Flash, Afrika Bambaata, Busy Bee, Grand Wizard Theodore and Deejay Jazzy Jay—all inspired by Disco King Mario and Chuck Chuck City and Big Mac Crew."

Zion and his homies closed their eyes as they bowed their heads to say a prayer for Disco King Mario.

Zion opened his eyes. "Grandmaster Flash is one of the greatest deejays that ever touched the turntable. Facts! I know some of the pioneers of hip-hop don't keep Disco King Mario name alive as they try to maintain their own legacy in hip-hop culture, but the streets of the Bronx will always know his impact in the imprint in the creation of hip-hop, toasting when the deejay controls the energy of B-Boys and the crowd. True hip-hop heads know the spirit of hip-hop was carved out in the ghetto and not corporate officers building."

Perneb looked outside of the restaurant window and saw an eagle flying. "It broke the Bronx's and hip-hop's hearts when Disco King Mario transcended, when he was only thirty-seven years old on May 21, 1994. We all have a reasonability to uphold Disco King Mario's spirit with the culture of hip-hop moving forward.

"Ayo, you know who I really miss in hip-hop?"

"Who, son?"

"I really miss Big L!"

"Ayo, we all miss the murderess lyrics of Big L. Nobody can touch his freestyle rhyme of rhythm. Big L was the reason I picked up the mic to honor his spirit!"

Jah stood up from his chair, saluting his big homie Quincy from Bronx River, who had taken him under his guidance when he was a teenager. He placed his right hand against the right side of his chest, symbolizing the deep respect he felt for Quincy in his heart.

Zion and his homies sat at a table near the door, feeling a cold draft as people entered and exited the café. Zion looked over the restaurant menu, changing the conversation. "Hotep, brother Khalid, you better hurry up to get your plane ticket for Ethiopia. September 11 is not that far away. You know Ethiopians celebrate every New Year's the immaculate conception of Ausar."

Zion and his friends asked the waitress to move them to another table. They were then escorted to a table in the back of the restaurant by a hostess named Fatima Zahir Aliya Ali. Zion noticed Fatima's accent and the way the structure of her skin tone reflected the sun's warmth on her rich, dark brown skin. He struck up a conversation with Fatima, learning that she was from Northern Sudan, specifically Darfur, and spoke her native language, Midob (Tid-n-aal). Zion read the menu in Arabic and placed their orders with Fatima in Tid-n-aal. She smiled at Zion and asked if he was Sudanese-Nubian.

"Hotep, queen. No. I am not, but my family, through my great-grandfather, is from Darfur."

"Hotep to you. It's so amazing to meet someone from the United States of America that can articulate the dialectic Tid-n-aal fluently. Tell me want else is so amazing about you?"

"I should be asking you the same."

"Excuse my manners. Let me properly introduce myself. My name is Zion El-Keif."

She smiled at him, blinking her eyes. "My name is Fatima Zahir Aliye Ali."

"Fatima, how long have you been living in Unites States?"

"Two weeks from today will make it one year since I've arrived in America."

"Congratulations on your soon to be one-year anniversary living in United States."

"Zion, how long did it take you to learn Tid-n-aal?"

""My family never lost our connection to the Semitic tongue of Tid-n-aal. Tid-n-aal has always been spoken in my family's home. It has been a part of my life since I was a child. My family has always traveled back and forth from America to Northern Kemet (Northern Sudan)."

Fatima became excited. "Zion, are you going to get on stage to recite a poem in Tid-n-aal? I would meri to hear you recite poetry in Tid-n-aal?"

Zion waved his hands and said, "No, I am not a poet. My friend Khalid Shabazz is going to recite a poem on stage."

"Zion, you're the first American I've met who knows how to speak Tid-n-aal," Fatima remarked.

"Fatima, you might not know this, but many Black people born in America, like myself, don't consider ourselves just American. We call ourselves African-American to connect our lineage to Mother Africa and the history we've created in America."

"That's interesting."

"Midob (Tid-n-aal) is a beautiful and captivating language. After completing my undergrad degree, I plan to further my education by studying Midob (Tid-n-aal) for two and a half years at the University of Khartoum in Sudan. I have distant relatives still living in Khartoum, about three hundred miles from the University of Khartoum. Perhaps we can continue this conversation over dinner with my family and take a stroll in the neighborhood tomorrow if you're not busy?"

Fatima smiled, bending her knees in a traditional greeting before walking away to give the chef their orders of food.

Chapter Thirteen

I Stand in My Revolutionary Square

Emcee Blazer, the emcee for the poetry jam, had a father from Jamaica and a mother from Cuba. His parents raised him and his two sisters in the East River Houses, located in East Harlem (Spanish Harlem). Emcee Blazer walked onto the stage, grabbing a microphone to introduce himself.

Emcee Blazer looked into the crowd. "What up? what up? To all my likeminded beloved brothers and sisters, I greet you all with peace. The Ancient words of Ase and Hotep. I am Emcee Blazer. Before we begin the poetry jam, I'd like to ask all my elders in the room, may I speak?"

The oldest elder in the room was a woman named Linda Davis, who was in her late sixties. She stood to her feet, looked directly at Emcee Blazer, and blew him a kiss. "My son, yes, you can speak."

Emcee Blazer bowed to one knee to honor Linda Davis. "I am asking for a moment of silence to pay homage to our murdered brothers: Botham Jean, Patrick Lyoya, and Joshua

Brown. We must never forget our sister, Atatiana Jefferson, from Texas."

Everyone lowered their heads, held the hands of the person next to them, and closed their eyes with empathy for Sandra Bland, Botham Jean, Joshua Brown, Atatiana Jefferson, George Floyd, Breonna Taylor, and many more Black brothers and sisters who had been murdered. After a moment of silence, people started opening their eyes, reflecting on the alarming rate of Black deaths.

Emcee Blazer spat poetic fire into the crowd. "Murderess assailants have continually killed our elders, sister, and brothers with bullets, their bare hands and knees, killing people. I remember in the 1980s when they killed Mrs. Eleanor Bumpurs, Willie Turks, Michael Stewart, Yusef Hawkins, and Michael Griffin. The killing of Black people continues to rage in the twenty-first century with the brutal murder of Botham Jean, Joshua Brown, Atatiana Jefferson, George Floyd, and Breonna Taylor physically, but their spirits must be upheld in each and every one of us gathered here. I would like to welcome everyone to Taste of Neteru. Today is the day when the warriors create a cypher to decide who are the warrior kings and warrior queen of poetry. I am going to start it off by wreaking the microphone with my ill poem titled 'I wanted You Since my Creation (Birth).'

"I wanted you since the creation of the universe, your melanin is each planet changing complexions. The touch of your skin is like a summer breeze, I hold you high into the universe, since our rebirth into this strange land, we have changed our names to make others feel comfortable with the Semitic tongues of our ancestors. You are my moon and always will be my queen goddess of the Nile. Nobody and nothing will come before you. I look outside, seeing all shades of the uniqueness of Black woman in the planets. I live for you: I look outside, seeing all shades of Blackness, I live for you, my queen. You are the light in my soul. I will never give you up. You are my Nile River, flowing deeper within my heart. The sun rises because of you. The sun sets in your presence. I will always forever stand by your side with my sword in my right hand to protect the art of your womb. I speak distant thoughts into my memory of you, my moon as we make passionate love…

"I feel your soul touching me everywhere as I sweat out my passion for you deep from left to right, up and down, vibrating throughout your spirit. East to west going deeper connecting within our Souls. Our minds move in one emotion searching for the prefect season for our bodies to produce a planet for our children. I have wanted you since my birth. You are the Mother of Creation; others have tried to take your Soul from the Universe. The Sky and the Earth is Creation of your reflection, my Moon. I am a warrior carrying the great dynasty of Memphis, sending our prayers to Mars, as I fight off evil forces on the battlefield with our souls to protect ancient sacred land of Thebes. Ungawa"

The crowd jumped to their feet, applauding Emcee Blazer as he completed his poem. The crowd continued applauding and snapping their fingers together, requesting an encore.

Emcee Blazer looked into the faces gathered. "Ungawa, ase family. Ase. Deejay, hit me with that hard-hitting bass! Yo, who's next on deck?"

The sound of the rhythm of the Afro beats playing in the background strengthened my energy!

The crowd had sat back in their seats, ordered drinks and food from the menu, and waited for the next poet to step on stage. Khalid Shabazz stood up, holding a piece of paper containing his written poem. He walked to the front to recite his poem, taking his place on stage.

Emcee Blazer handed Khalid the microphone, and looked into Khalid's eyes, noticing he was a little nervous, and smiled. He then spoke with a strong Uptown confident swag. "Mo, whatever you do, don't drop the mic. Relax, brother, you got this."

Khalid Shabazz cleared his throat as he looked around the crowd gathered around the room. He took a deep breath. Then, he opened his mouth, speaking with confidence with a strong bass voice with an East London, British accent. "Hotep, family. My name is Khalid Shabazz. I want to say big ups to my family and friends in West London. I have written a poem from my ka. I have written this poem with a deep desire in my Ka that I will recite to you all today. My poem from my heart a capella. The title of the poem is 'Spirituality of our Love.'

"I desire a unique love that chant messages into my spirit that grows old (wisdom) in my spirit. I desire a love that speaks to me every day, every night waking me up with every morning staring, kissing and touching me with the connection of her eyes. I desire a love that I don't have to chase after, a love that I call my own. Sharing my dreams with her as she tells me about her deepest desires from her spirit. No more wishing for love only praying our spirits connect with each word we recite. No lie will define our love, each experience we had separately before meeting each other will bring us closer together to understand why our souls were chosen to be together. Telling her stories of my yesterday as I ran into the spirituality of her soul today...

"With each moment I stand outside turning my wife into my wisdom, waiting for her with my eyes and arms wide open. Speaking enchanting tongues to Amen'Ra and our ancient ancestors, feeling their spirits sending messages in the strong wind from the east that our love is a spirituality that will serve and only be faithful to tomorrow's birth of our stars that turn into our children. I feel your touch even when you're a million miles away. My love will never be too far from you. My love will stay in my heart and soul. When I think about you, my thoughts are captivated with impregnated spirits of higher heights of our love!

"I pray Amen'Ra protects our spirituality of love as we fly and climax as our true spirituality of love reaches infinity. With wisdom, we will always be spiritual when it comes to love: we share for today and a prayer for tomorrow."

The crowd stood to their feet, congratulating Khalid Shabazz for his performance. Emcee Blazer shook his head, smiling, and clapped his hands together. More poets stepped on stage, reciting their poetry to the audience gathered around the café. Lyah sat in her seat, listening to the poetry and sipping her green tea from her cup, waiting for her and Baraka's breakfast order. She stared at Baraka across from the table, observing him with his head down as he looked through pictures. Baraka began taking one of his cameras out of his camera bag and looked up to find Lyah staring at him. He moved his seat next to Lyah and showed her pictures he had taken years ago during his summer internship after graduating from high school, when he was seventeen years old, during his trip to Colombia.

Baraka looked at Lyah and said, "Lyah, have I ever shown you these pictures of my internship when I spent the summer in Cali, Colombia?"

"No, I've never seen these pictures of your trip to Colombia before."

"Before I went to Colombia, I conducted extensive research about the diverse history, people, and cultures of Colombia. During my first few days in Cali, Colombia, I noticed that people from different tribes easily identified each other through tribal facial features and marks. I was profoundly influenced by the richness of the fertile soil I encountered, capturing the unique essence of Colombia. The dialect of Spanish and Creole spoken there is vastly different from that of other Central and South American countries I have visited during my travels. A woman told me that tribes can identify each other through braiding pattern styles. Afrikan-Colombians have an irresistible and primeval connection to the indigenous soil of Colombia. They have created hairstyles inspired by the experiences they endured during the period of slavery.

"When women sat in their slave cabins, they secretly gathered with other Indigenous-Afrikans around the circle of fire. They had combed their children's hair after restless nights of suffering, worked day and night, felt aches and pains from being tortured by their so-called slave masters. Their hands and feet had remained restless from working on slave plantations and in gold mines.

"The terror of the reminders of the lashes on their bodies from the whip enhanced their desire to regain their freedom. Mothers had braided their children's hairstyles, using codes and signals to indicate that they were planning an escape and sharing escape routes with other Indigenous-Afrikans. Men and women who were enslaved had hidden gold and seeds to help them survive and find refuge after they escaped, relaying messages between other slaves in Colombia."

Baraka shook his head and licked his lips. "I felt the Spirit of Ma'at breathing into my soul ever since I was in Colombia for two and one-half weeks. I took about a thousand pictures with my cameras. If I would've stayed in Colombia for another two more weeks, I would've taken two thousand more pictures."

"Baraka, when are you going to finally open the photography and art school you always talking about?"

"I am planning to open my first photography and art school next year to teach Kemet children to use their dreams to create a canvas through the camera with each picture they will capture. I feel it's my destiny to teach KEMET children. Sometimes, when I am capturing pictures, I feel the wind blowing into my Spirit of Ma'at. I almost had enough money to open the school, but I decided to buy a house first to create more stability through my home equity. The book of Tehut teaches, 'Everything you need, all comes to you at the prefect time.' Moving forward, Lyah, how would you feel if I decide to renovate the basement to create two small classes for a film and art studios?"

Fatima walked back to Zion and his warrior brothers' table, observing them in a deep cypher, discussing the Seventh Hermetic Principle of Gender. Zion bowed his head to begin praying before speaking to his friend, Khalid Shabazz.

Zion lifted his head, looked at Khalid, and said, "Hotep, Brother Shabazz, Gender is in everything. Even flowers have masculine and feminine principles. Gender manifests on all planes. The Universal law embodies the truth that there is gender manifestation in everything."

Khalid sipped on his drink and replied, "Hotep, Zion, true indeed. There is not one aspect of life that the masculine and feminine principles are not manifest into birth to create life. This is correct for all three planes. The physical plane, the mental plane, and the Spiritual plane. On the physical plane, the principle manifests as sexual. On the higher planes, it takes a higher form, but the principle is always the same. It is impossible for creation to take place on the physical, mental, or Spiritual planes without these laws. Everything has a dualistic concept of yin and yang."

Zion observed Fatima approaching the table with the food they had ordered.

Zion took a book out of his book bag, placed it on the table, and then placed his hands on the table, saying, "All creation has a balance. Hotep, Fatima. What are your thoughts on The Seventh Hermetic principles?"

Fatima placed the plates on the table. "My Kemetic knowledge teaches me silence is of great profit. An abundance of speech, a life of creation. No one has reached full knowledge, so listen and heed, or wisdom to avoid when evil is spoken. For truth, like the sunlight, shines above all cruises for proficiency. I read this book the other day; it is written in Kemetic and titled 'Everything You Need Will Come to You."

"Fatima, I am impressed with your vast knowledge of the Kemetic laws and principles. Our great ancestors have given us all Ma'at!"

"I am also intrigued by the fascination of the power of your Spiritual presence," Zion said with a smile to Fatima.

Zion stared at each of his comrades with pride. He introduced them to Fatima as Perneb, Jah, Khaseekhemwy, and Khalid. Then, Zion began reading the book to himself.

Everyone greeted Fatima with "Hotep."

Khalid asked him about the book he was reading. Zion showed him the cover of the book and told Khalid, "It is *The Africans Who Wrote the Bible* by Nana Banchie Darkwah, Ph. D."

Fatima shyly looked at everyone and said, "Hotep, you all remind me of back home in my village, where men would gather around when Ra (the Sun) went down, discussing matters of the day."

Khaseekhemwy nodded at Fatima and told her, "In the States, we sometimes gather on street corners. Fatima, tomorrow we are gathering to hear our Spiritual Teachers Dr. Ashra and Mother Meira Kwesi lecturing about Universal Kemetic Spirituality, history, culture, and civilization. The lecture will focus on Kemet's first ruler, Hotepsekhenwy of the second dynasty."

Fatima looked at Khaseekhemwy and said, "Before I give you an answer, Zion, how does your Ka balance in truth, justice, morality, and righteousness."

Zion, with a serious look on his face, responded, "I didn't always know this, but to continue my journey, I had to gain a greater understanding of the deity within my Ka (Soul). When I study to understand the Law of Heru: 'You have the power but not the right to ignore God's Law. Choose to follow the law of God with the love and joy that grows out of understanding, wisdom, and the power of God's Spirit will follow through your being."

Fatima looked at him and said, "Zion, I am glad you are coming to understand the Aat (Great one) within yourself."

Zion continued, "The Law of Sebek: 'It is not what you think or what you affirm. It is who is thinking and affirming. Are you a human or a divine being?"

Chapter Fourteen

We are the Nu (Black) Diamond
Cipher of Meri (Love)

Emcee Blazer stood on stage, commanding the complete attention of everyone in the café as he spoke, "Mastery of the power of words... Ungawa... I greet you all with the ancient words of Hotep and Ase, family. On July 28, two months from today's date, I am sponsoring a cultural event and a one-night-only R&B concert with a special guest who will perform all his greatest hits on the night before we leave on August 1. The tour will be first class; we will be boarding the bus that will take us to Washington, D.C. When we arrive in D.C., we will stay in a five-star hotel."

The waitstaff went from table to table, handing out flyers to everyone in attendance. "On July 28, we are taking a two-day tour of the African-American Museum in Washington, D.C. After touring the African-American Museum for two days, on the third day, we are going to unify our spirits and come together with brothers and sisters from the

DMV (Washington, D.C., Maryland, and Virginia). In the afternoon, we are going to gather at Sankofa Video Books and Café to listen to a joint lecture on holistic health and Spiritual healing by Queen Afua and an extensive lecture on the research of Africology by Professor James Smalls."

A lady in her thirties seated in the back of the café interrupted Emcee Blazer, yelling out, "Blazer, who is the special R&B artist that will perform?"

"Word up, queen! You are going to enjoy the special guest I was able to secure to perform. Yo, yo, family, our Moorish Brother R&B singer Jaheim is going to perform."

"Oh yeah, I am going to D.C. to see my play husband Jaheim perform. I cannot wait to hear him sing 'Always Come Back.' I am going to ask him if he wants to come back home with me."

People in the café started laughing at what the woman said.

The lady said out loud, not caring who heard her, "What? I am not playing. Jaheim is coming home with me!"

Baraka touched Lyah's hand and said to her, "Lyah, we should take a trip to Washington, D.C. to take a tour of the African-American Museum and go to check out Queen Afua and Professor James Smalls at Sankofa Video, Books, and Café."

"I have all of Jaheim's albums. Jaheim is my favorite singer. I can't wait to hear him sing his songs 'Remarkable,' oh yeah, and 'Struggle Love.' I love all his songs. We definitely have to go."

"Cool, I have family living in D.C. That will be a nice trip."

Baraka and Lyah looked at the flyer, going over the tour schedule. The waitress approached their table, introducing herself. Baraka ordered a pineapple mojito, and Lyah ordered an aguas frescas drink. Eight minutes later, the waitress returned, placing napkins and two straws on the table as she set Lyah's and Baraka's drinks down.

Baraka sipped on his drink, and Lyah looked at him, enjoying the taste of the pineapple mojito.

Lyah smiled into Baraka's eyes. "Baraka, you always talk about planning to open your own photography and art school. Remember the Law of Auset? 'Prepare to sacrifice become the vessel of God on earth, and you will, in turn, receive everything."

Baraka held Lyah's hands and took a deep breath. "Lyah, I feel in my spirit I have to do this as it is written in The Law of Geb: 'Know that from heaven you will return, seek not enduring works on earth."

Lyah stared at him. "I see, Baraka, you are taking your Kemetic lessons seriously to enhance your faith in yourself."

"Lyah, I am learning The Law of Heru Khut: 'Know that God neither punishes nor rewards nor protect that you will have the comfort of controlling these yourself."

Several people entered Taste of the Neteru Café to order organic delicious food and listen to great poets recite their poetry on stage.

Lyah gazed at the stage, silently moving her lips as the rhythms of her poetry flowed through her mind. Baraka stared into Lyah's eyes, recognizing that she was in a trance, composing a poem from the depths of her soul.

Baraka caressed Lyah's elbow, and said, with confidence in his heart, "Lyah, it's your time. You must allow the poetry in your Ka to speak for you."

Lyah looked at him, smiling, and blew a meri kiss to him, which he received in his heart. She stood to her feet and walked onto the stage, holding the microphone in her hands. Lyah allowed her spirit to lead her before reciting her poem. "Hotep, family. I am a virgin to the stage but not to poetry. I was sitting with my husband, Baraka, listening to the beautiful poets. I became inspired to freestyle a poem that is written in my Ka."

Lyah took a deep breath and looked at Emcee Blazer as he stood offstage next to a conga drum.

Lyah turned toward the side of the stage and spoke, "Brother, can I get a conga drumbeat to synchronize the rhythm of my poetry with the audience? Baraka, I meri you, baby! I dedicate my poem to our sisters Atatiana Jefferson and Breonna Taylor. Brothers and sisters, I hope you all enjoy my poem titled 'We Are a Strong Black Nation of Warrior Goddesses and Warrior Kings.'

"Ungawa, Ungawa, Ungawa...We must build a strong Black nation of warrior goddess and warrior kings to continue on our great-great-great grandparents of the blessing bestowed within all Kemetic warriors through our inheritance from our Ka (Souls). Rise up like the Ra (Sun) Kemet man, stand up and fight! fight! I call on you the fathers and sons of the Universe to look into your warrior queen goddess eyes crying out for ancient Kemetic warriors to protect her.

"Look deep into her battered skin don't deny that you see the bruises from pain in her Ka (Soul)? She wants you to fight for her with all you're might and strengthen in your Spirit. I speak from my heart to all Kemetic ancient warriors. A strong Black nation is forming all around us in the room with Ra guiding the Moon and Stars of strong Black warrior kings. Warrior goddess and our babies.

"Our Universal Ka (Soul) must unite to give rebirth to a future strong Black nation of spiritual warriors and scholars. I hear our children chanting in the Wind to Mother Afrika for ancient knowledge for direction to the land of our ancestors birthplace?

"In my prayers at night, I see our children bathe in the Ancient Waters of the Nile River.

"My sisters and I patiently wait for you; Black man listen to the Universe shacking from the graves of our ancient ancestors. Each prayer I pray I always complete by saying "I honor your Ka (Souls) waiting for our nation of powerful warriors for tomorrow's freedom.

"Within my prayers, I know our ancient ancestors are teaching me the history of the past that will give rebirth to my future sons and daughters. Black men it's your obligation to uphold the Kemet Nu nation with your spirit to fight as revolutionaries to revenge the deaths of all Black women murder by bloodthirsty barbarians."

The crowd was astonished, and everyone began clapping with excitement at Lyah's profound spoken words. Baraka walked on stage and hugged her tightly. They walked back to their table.

"Baraka, my hands are sweaty. I was so nervous on stage."

"Girl, you did your thang on stage today. I am really enjoying myself with you, Lyah. This is a beautiful café. We should make this our new meri place. Lyah, I am so proud to call you my wife, my queen!"

"I truly meri you, Baraka."

Baraka blew a kiss to Lyah, saying to her, "I meri the way you say my name. You know I was given the name Baraka Kwame Imamu Asari-Dokubo by my father at birth, after the iconic activist, poet, theatre director, producer, and writer Amiri Baraka. My father would always tell me when I was a child, when he felt I was losing focus, 'Son, I gave you the name Baraka Kwame Imamu Asari-Dokubo to bestow the blessings and gifts of our Mother Creator, Father Creator, and all our great ancestors. You have the duty to uphold and live up to the strength and power of your chosen name, Baraka

Kwame Imamu Asari-Dokubo. Baraka, the truth of your gifts and talents will create the audacity of your destiny. You must declare that your destiny lives inside of you."

Perneb looked around the restaurant, marveled at the structural design of the interior, and felt the energy of the spirit of Tehuti cycling around the room.

Staring at Fatima, Perneb said, "Fatima, many sisters and brothers will attend the lecture to gain superior knowledge and reach a higher level of Tehuti. Tehuti teaches us that power lies in ideas recorded as facts or data in cosmic memory. When necessary, this cosmic memory can reveal its ancient wisdom to those who call upon it. His energy is said to break through mental barriers, allowing information to become known and revealing secrets or lost and forgotten ideas. Tehuti assists in the discovery of lost knowledge, but he communicates more directly with our minds in a methodology to dispel mental confusion."

Fatima thought carefully before answering Perneb's question. "Perneb, the God Tehuti is a spiritual and intellectual master that many believe has power over the Universe."

Perneb nodded, understanding her response. "Fatima, my Kemet family, we build a cypher of conscious knowledge every time we unite with the power of our ancestors."

Zion turned his attention to Perneb. "My brother Perneb is speaking facts. Khalid, are you going to bring your queen Wakemah to the lecture tomorrow?"

Khalid looked around at the gathered crowd in the café and said, "In the spirit of the great Imhotep, I have to bring my wife, Princess."

Fatima looked at him with curiosity and asked, "Khalid, you are married?"

Khalid nodded. "Yes, I am. Princess has asked me for a long time, 'When are we going to go to a Dr. Ashra and Meria Kwesi lecture?' Fatima, you should come to hear Dr. Ashra and Meria Kwesi lecture. I will introduce you to my queen, Princess."

Fatima looked at Khalid and smiled. "I would like to meet your wife. Khalid, what is your understanding of the father of medicine, the great Imhotep?"

"I am in my second year of medical school. Several times, I wanted to quit medical school, but my desire to follow in the great lineage of Great Imhotep (He comes in peace), who was the chief architect at Saqqara, Kemet, for the step pyramid Djoser (Djesser), kept me going. Great Imhotep (He comes in peace) revolutionized medicine around the globe in the twenty-seventh century B.C. I have intensified my studies to become a physician because Great Imhotep was a genius.

"Imhotep is the inspirational reason why I chose to be a medical physician. He was a scientist who wrote prodigious medical books on medicine and authored several medical works. The Great Imhotep is the author of the Edwin Smith papyrus, claiming he discovered hundreds of medical cures, actually discovering cures for over two hundred diseases. The Great Imhotep defined more than ninety anatomical terms and described forty-eight injuries. He founded a school of medicine in Ancient Memphis, Kemet, known as Asklepion, which remained famous for over two thousand years. All this occurred 2,200 years before the mythology of Greece.

"The Great Imhotep's medical discovery work was plagiarized by Edwin Smith who proclaimed he discovered these medical cures. Great Imhotep actually was the real medical physician/scientist that researched hundreds of medical cures for diseases and acute pain in people bodies. Great Imhotep is and will remain my inspiration with his genius diagnoses and holistic treatment to cure people's illnesses, encompassing over two hundred diseases, including fifteen abdominal disorders, eleven treatments for bladder infections, ten for rectal issues, twenty-nine for eye problems, and eighteen for skin, hair, nails, and tongue conditions. Great Imhotep treated tuberculosis, gallstones, appendicitis, gout, and arthritis. Great Imhotep crafted and mastered instruments for surgical procedures. He was a multi-genius, extracting medicine from plants to holistically cure diseases that afflict mind, body, Spirit, and Soul, embracing the deities of the Universe as the falcon embraces the wind when it flies with broad wings. The Greeks called him Aesculapius; his name is used in modern times when medical physicians take the Hippocratic oath to become doctors."

Fatima looked at Zion, smiling at him. "I will go to the lecture. I am excited and pleased to go."

A husband and wife walked into the Taste of Netru Café to order food to take home. The woman looked down at her two-year-old son in a stroller, and she was five months pregnant with their second child. She gently placed her hand on her belly as she perused the menu while her husband took their son out of the stroller and playfully tickled his son. The two-year-old boy giggled and asked his father to stop, and the man smiled at his son's laughter. Afterward, the woman placed their son back in the stroller, and her husband carried the food in a bag. He opened the café's front door to allow his wife to exit with their son.

Baraka and Lyah sat at their table, smiling and observing the man with his pregnant wife and son.

Baraka lowered his head, feeling the weight on his shoulders. He said, "All my brothers and sisters have children."

"I know, Baraka, I know. My youngest sister, Tyerah, called me last week, overjoyed with excitement, telling me she was two months pregnant."

Baraka nodded. "That's good for Tyerah and her husband."

The waitress returned to their table and asked if they were ready to order. Lyah and Baraka looked over the menu and placed their orders for a delicious meal. The waitress wrote down their orders on a notepad before walking away to inform the chef of their orders.

Baraka and Lyah continued their conversation while waiting for their food.

Lyah looked into his eyes. "She asked me to plan a baby shower for her."

Baraka tilted his head, appearing as if he didn't understand what she was saying.

"Uh, did you forget already that we were talking about Tyerah a few minutes ago?"

"No, I didn't forget. I remember. Go ahead, Lyah, I am listening to you."

"Tyerah asked me to plan a baby shower for her." Lyah paused, looking down. "Oh, Mighty Creator, please forgive me. I feel so ashamed. I do want my sister to have a baby. Why am I not happy for her?"

"Lyah, don't feel ashamed. You are still dealing with your own pain. I meri you, Lyah. You are my world."

"Tell the truth to me, Baraka? Be honest with me? I know you want to have children so much. When we first got married, all you talked about was us meri (loving) each other and having a house full of children."

Baraka looked around the café at people enjoying their meals. "I am hungry; I wonder where the waitress is with our food?"

Lyah expressed her anticipation. "We don't talk about us having children anymore; we are silent when we are around each other. You stopped talking to me. We are silent."

"I do talk with you about us having children." Baraka defended himself.

"No, you don't talk about us having children. You only want to talk about the miscarriages and Mutulu being stillborn. There is a difference."

"Yeah, when I bought our house, I thought it would be full of children running around, laughing, and playing."

Lyah frowned. "I am so sorry."

"Sorry for what? I already told you the miscarriages and Mutulu being stillborn were not your fault. Each argument we have is met with silence to avoid what we really want to say to each other. What do you want to say to me, Lyah?"

"What if I cannot have children?" Lyah asked.

"You know I love you, Lyah."

"What happens to our love if I can never give birth to a healthy child? Answer my question, Baraka. What happens to our lives then?"

"I've always felt the desire to have children to complete my soul. Lyah, I am not giving up on us. Our Almighty Creator has a plan for our love. I've been praying and waiting for a blessing to help our union of love since our prince, Mutulu Diara Asari-Dokubo, passed away." Baraka reassured her.

Lyah wiped a tear forming in her left eye. "I have been praying, too, for our love."

"Let's make a promise to ourselves to stop fighting and arguing, to create a new Akhet (season of flood) cycle in our relationship with better communication. I have real love for you, Lyah."

"I love you too much to see you leave, Baraka. I want you to know that my love is unique. I love with diligence."

"That's why I chose you to be my wife."

Lyah giggled. "Baraka, you didn't choose me. Our spirits chose for us to be in love."

Baraka agreed. "Lyah, you are absolutely right; our destiny was sealed for us to be husband and wife. That's why I will always love you forever, Lyah!"

"Baraka, keep saying that you love me every single day. I believe your actions are true."

"Your soul is like a jewel to my spirit. Lyah, we have great chemistry together."

"I know. The essence of time is indefinite. Neither you nor I can surrender or lose the purpose of our existence together. Baraka, if you are really serious about meri (loving) me, I need a renewed ankh (sworn oath) of commitment. Your voice carries into the winds of Deja. Last night, I looked into the skies, visualizing that you would ask for my ankh."

"Lyah, I've always told you I love you."

"If you're truly in love with me, don't just say it; prove your love to me every day," Lyah challenged.

"Lyah, you are a blessed one (Akhu). I would give my life to save yours. You know that, Lyah."

Prove your ankh through your Jb by dedicating your life to Mother Creator and Father Creator."

Baraka kissed the palms of her hands. "I have proven my ankh every day of how far my meri reaches for you. I hustle day to day on my job for us, I'll do anything for you. I made you, my wife. What else can I sacrifice to prove my Jb?"

"I put my meri for you first, placing our meri in my inner Ka where nobody but Neter (Most High Amen'Ra), you and I can reach. I desire you with my Ka and Spirit attached. I search your Ka trying to find out if your Spirit reaches the same Spirituality as my Ka. I pray for our meri."

"I pray every day, four times a day, with you in my Ka."

"I pray Amen'Ra hears my prayers. I pray for Ra's blessing for you every day because I meri you."

Chapter Fifteen

Indigenous Universal Nu (Black) Womb

Baraka looked up at the Ra (Sun) and said to Lyah, "Our love is strengthening abundantly. We have a chemistry through our Ka that no one can destroy."

"My king, I entrust my future in your eyes, communicating with you in the ancient Semitic spiritual tongues of Medu Neter (Words of Nature).".

"I truly love you!" Baraka declared. "Lyah, when we are strong together, we are creating a powerful manifestation of a great king and queen, aren't we?"

After finishing their meals, Baraka and Lyah sat quietly, enjoying the background music and the beautiful scenery of the Taste of Netru Café. They watched people conversing as they ate their meals, and Lyah couldn't help but giggle, leaving behind thoughts of her past pain.

"Raka, how was your meal?"

"I thoroughly enjoyed my chicken and waffles. The food was delicious. If we were at home right now, I'd be licking the plate clean. Mmm, the food was really good." Baraka smiled with satisfaction.

Lyah laughed. "You are so crazy."

"How was your meal?"

"The food was fabulous. Baraka, what time is it now?"

Baraka looked at this watch. "Wow, time went by so fast. It's already 6:34 p.m. Lyah are you ready to go home?"

Silence spoke for their Ka (Souls). Lyah took a deep breath.

"Lyah, we can't go home now."

"I know. I don't want this moment to come to an end. I'm not done having fun. Raka, do you want to go to a movie on 125th Street?"

"No, I want to keep hearing your voice without the interruption of our Ka (Souls) becoming silent. Where do you want to go after we leave here?"

"Let's just walk and allow our hearts to find a place that our Ka (Souls) can direct our paths."

"Lyah, you've shown me the best of myself since we've been together. I'm ready to show you that you are my queen, right now."

Baraka stood to his feet. "Mrs. Asari-Dokubo, are you ready to go?"

Lyah looked into Baraka's eyes with a deep passionate stare. "Of course, I am ready, my king. You know what?"

"What?"

"Baraka, you will always be my boo. I will go anywhere you want to go Mr. Asari-Dokubo."

Baraka paid for his and Lyah's meal with cash, leaving the waitress a nice tip on the table. They walked out of Taste Netru Café, strolling down the street, carefully listening to each other as they conversed. They stopped to listen to a man named Brother Jamari, who was in his forties, standing on the block, teaching knowledge to people in the streets about politics, quoting Jamil Abdullah Al-Amin.

Brother Jamari stood in his square, saying, "The system mandating the actions of the individual doesn't determine how this country will function. We all must relearn the systemic structure of how politicians run their propaganda campaigns in public one way but when they are elected, they rule the people another way. Freedom ain't free. You cannot bomb people to death by peace. You can only bomb people to surrender or fight a war with domestic myths of genocidal wars against themselves or international terrorism."

A Brother named Jacob, dressed in fly gear and in his early twenties, moved through the crowd that had gathered on the block, listening to Brother Jamari. Jacob moved faster, passing the crowd. Brother Jamari noticed him as he attempted to converse with Jacob. Jacob looked at him and said, "I don't have no time to stand here with you as you attempt to hustle some two-bit 1990's knowledge. I am moving in my square, maintaining my cultural knowledge of self."

Brother Jamari replied, "So, Black man, you ain't gotta listen to me. I am only trying to reconstruct your mindset and bless you with real Ancient wisdom to build greater cyphers with young Brothers like yourself."

Jacob retorted, "Yeah, that's what you're saying now, until you get the guap."

Brother Jamari responded, "I am an educator, not a hustler. I am a licensed college professor. I teach knowledge to weaponize our people for the war ahead."

Baraka and Lyah listened to Jamari for a while before writing down his contact information as they walked away to enjoy their day.

Baraka held Lyah's left hand. "For a long time, I hesitated to admit the truth, but I knew the first time I told you 'I meri you,' you were meant to be the best of my meri as my wife at a traditional Kemetic wedding. With each kiss of your lips, I want to continue sharing my world with you."

"Baraka, are you telling me you want to renew our wedding vows in a traditional Kemetic wedding? Not because you are afraid of losing me?"

"I want to renew our wedding vows this weekend. Mother Creator and Father have created me to be a great warrior. I need you to forgive me for my past mistakes."

Lyah looked at him with a questioning expression. "What do you need me to forgive you for?"

"Lyah, just meri me unconditionally? Promise me, you will continue being my wife?"

Lyah looked at him. "Baraka, are you ready to ask me again to be your wife and you will be a father to the chosen children of Sudan that nutritious their Ka in the Blue Nile?'

"Lyah give me your hand?" Baraka reached out his right hand. "I will never give up on you. I'll do anything for you to keep meri me."

"What about our fears?"

"When I hold you in my arms, I feel reborn. My Ka is reunited with our Ancient Spirituality," Baraka expressed.

"Baraka, before I met you, I was ready to forget about meri, thinking it would never happen to me again. I used to stare at you when we started dating, wondering why you came into my life. I buried my feelings, believing I had to protect myself against love. I remember when I was pregnant with Mutulu, my holistic doula and I were doing everything to ensure I would have a healthy pregnancy.

"Mutulu would wake me up in the middle of the night moving around inside of my Universal Black Womb finding his own way of communicating with me. The day of my labor, I knew something was wrong because I didn't feel Mutulu moving around my womb. I called my holistic doula on the telephone telling her I cannot feel Mutulu in my womb. She told me not to panic as she hung up the telephone arriving at the house ten minutes later accessing my options giving me her professional opinion from a balance unconditional physical, mental, peaceful, emotional and Spiritual telling me to go to the hospital."

Lyah looked down as she started to cry. "Weeks and months passed since that day. Since we lost Mutulu, I've rushed out the front door of the house in the morning to go to work throughout the day and then come home and lay in bed at night, thinking how much pain I carry inside of me day after day. How much more do I have to give? I am so tired of this pain living inside of me."

Standing in front of the Caribbean Culture Center/African Diaspora Institute on 125th Street in Harlem, Lyah reached out her hand to hold Baraka's hand as they entered the lobby of the Caribbean Culture Center/African Diaspora Institute before walking around. They looked around and saw promotions for future cultural events at the Caribbean Center/African Diaspora Institute. Lyah and Baraka began conversing with a professional dancer named Jennifer Scott, who was two months pregnant. Jennifer handed Lyah and Baraka two invitations to a play that she and her dance troupe would be performing in honor of the Nicholas Brothers, Dandridge Sisters, Bill "Bojangles" Robinson, and Count Basie on stage at the Dance Theatre of Harlem next month. Lyah and Baraka thanked Jennifer for the invitation to her performance at the Dance Theatre of Harlem.

Lyah exchanged telephone numbers with Jennifer, smiling and hugging her while congratulating Jennifer on her pregnancy. Afterward, she and Baraka walked through of the Caribbean Culture Center/African Diaspora Institute's front door.

As they strolled through Harlem, a man walked up to them, handing them a flyer for a Juneteenth celebration parade in Harlem. Lyah and Baraka continued walking, and as they did, Lyah looked at Baraka with tears forming in her eyes.

Inhaling a deep breath of fresh air, she said, "Baraka, I know we've talked about this already, but I have to know. Am I still a mother after losing our babies? Sometimes I wonder if I will ever become a mother again."

Baraka hugged Lyah and then wiped her tears with the palm of his hands. "Yes, you are still a mother, Lyah. When we suffered the miscarriage of Mutulu for days and months I endured the pain in my mind and Jb in silence trying to be resilient for the both of us. Three weeks ago, I woke up feeling pain in my chest and the right side of my face, making it difficult for me to breath and sleep at night. The pain wouldn't go away until I released the pain that I was hiding from. Two weeks ago, I look outside of the window tire of not being able to recognizes the moonlight from the morning Ra (Sun) light. I know I had to release the pain to free myself. I realized if I stay in the darkness for too long hiding from the truth. My chest pain will only lead me more into the darkness and the mirror will only show my reflection crying out tears."

The crowd on 128th street was moving with an enteric rhythm and momentum, full of sensation. Baraka faced Lyah, holding her hands against his lips and repeatedly kissing Lyah's hands.

"Yes, Lyah, you are a mother. We are parents. We cleansed our Ka (Souls) together by renewing our wedding vows."

"You are right; we needed to cleanse our Ka to create a new beginning. Baraka, do you really think renewing our wedding vows will help us have more children?"

"I have no doubt in my mind that we will continue our journey of being parents."

Lyah looked up as Baraka spoke.

"Wait, wait…please don't give up on me. Every time you talk and smile into my eyes you breathe life into my Jb. Don't give up on us. I need you. Your fears of your past Akh (relationships) and the miscarriage keep allowing you to keep looking through the rear review mirror blocking your revision. Lyah, I am here. I will always be here for you. Lyah, are you ready to free yourself of the pain you refuse to forgive yourself of that you didn't cause?"

They proceeded to walk along 125th Street, heading toward Adam Clayton Powell Jr. Boulevard, all the while enjoying the soulful music and observing the people of Harlem as they conversed and reveled in their surroundings. Along the way, Lyah made a brief stop to purchase essential oils, two shea butter products from Senegal, and three lavender incense sticks from a vendor situated on 125th Street. Meanwhile, Baraka glanced across the street and noticed one of his acquaintances selling a hip-hop remix CD right in front of the Apollo Theater.

Baraka looked at Lyah before crossing the street. "Lyah, I'll be right back."

"Raka, wait? I see that lady vendor across the street selling sage. Grab three sages for me, please?"

"Alright."

Lyah carried on with her shopping, and as she did, she spotted a fifteen-year-old teenage boy who stood at an impressive height of six-foot-eight, dribbling his basketball skillfully on the sidewalk. He was clearly practicing and working on improving his dribbling techniques to secure a spot on his high school's basketball varsity team.

While Baraka engaged in conversation with his friend, Lyah crossed the street to join him. When she reached his side, she gazed into his eyes (Soul) with a smile and said, "Baraka, I'm here with you now."

Lyah continued to explore her surroundings, attentively listening to the voices of the people in the bustling city streets. During her observations, she noticed a man who was strolling at a leisurely pace, capturing photographs of the streets and the vibrant Nu (Black) community of Harlem. Many Nu (Black) individuals hurried past him on the sidewalk, striving to maintain the vigor of their momentum in their daily lives.

As more Nu (Black) people passed by him, the man persisted in taking pictures of both the people and the streets.

At one point, a Nu (Black) man bumped aggressively into the photographer's shoulder, seemingly attempting to snatch the camera from him. "What up? what up? Get that camera out of my face! You are acting like a fuckin tourist."

"Yo, man, is you going to keep standing here, or you going to keep moving?"

"Nobody is stopping your movement!"

"You are walking too slow. Move out of the way. I am on a mission, get out of the way now! You are stopping my guap movement!"

Lyah walked down the street seeing to men arguing face to face as a woman attempted to defuse the augment.

One of the men said to the other man, "You better close your mouth while I am eying your chick! Keep fucking with me, I'll make your wife my future baby mother."

"Fuck you!"

"Ox, don't worry. After I am done, I'll send her back home to you."

"Whatever, man, I die before I let you take what is mine! What up! Yeah, you know what time it is, fucking with me!"

"I am only going to tell you this one time. You better keep—"

The other guy interrupted him. "You got five seconds to get out of my face. Word!"

"You know who I am! My name is covered with blood in these streets. Yo, yo keep my name out of your mouth!"

"Yo, son, pull up to 155th; you know where I'll be whenever you ready!"

Lyah turned the corner before the one of the men pulled out gun to prove his point. Baraka looked from afar, seeing the concerning look on Lyah's face. He started running to her to protect her against any danger.

"When I was younger the streets of Harlem were my cultural center of knowledge and discovery. Harlem is still the cultural center that inspires me to be a fashion designer."

Baraka listened to Lyah speak as they stood in front of the Apollo Theater. Lyah felt the strap of her right high heel shoe loosening. She bent down to fix it, and Baraka suddenly knelt in front of her, wrapping his arms around her waist and kissing Lyah's Universal Womb to heal her pain.

"Before I met you, I searched and searched, but I knew, Lyah, there was no need to search any further after I met you. I just knew my search was complete when I met you. Lyah, we will get through this journey together."

"Let's not stop now; we should keep walking."

Baraka and Lyah looked for a quiet place to listen to each other's Ka (Souls). They walked to Madison Avenue, East 120th Street, entering Marcus Garvey Park, where they saw people throughout the park exercising and families having cookouts. They decided to sit at a bench under a two-hundred-thirty-three-year-old Royal Poinciana tree. Lyah quieted her spirit, listening to nature as the wind and birds sang to her in sequences.

Baraka looked at Lyah, seeing how happy she was, and said to her, "We will name our next son Taharqa Asari-Dokubo, to honor one of our greatest Nubian-Sudanese warrior ancestors, King Taharqa, who led his Warrior Nation Napata to reclaim the Ancient nation of Kemet, against the Assyrians, in defense of his second cousins, the original Israelites. Lyah, I know Mother Creator and Father Creator have healed your womb to allow you and me to have more children."

"Baraka, the wind is blowing stronger as I feel my Spirit reenergizing. I cannot wait to celebrate Harlem Week this year."

"Harlem Week was a tradition and festival in my family home when I was growing up. The tradition of Harlem Week was always celebrated since my parents first met each other at the first Harlem Week in 1974."

"Baraka, the sky looks so beautiful. I am understanding more of our divine purpose. Spiritually, we are a manifestation of spiritual light and life!"

"Six years ago, I started my journey of Kemetic Spirituality with a blank canvas, just a blank canvas. Lyah, I don't know any other way to tell you, I meri you, but through the way I feel. With you here by my side, I know we share the essence of a Kemetic meri through each of our prayers."

A bright reddish leaf from the Royal Poinciana tree fell to the ground. Lyah smiled, looking at the leaf as it lay on the ground. She stared with an ecstatic, blissful expression on her face. A man named Charles Joiner walked up to them, holding a saxophone in his hands. He introduced himself to Baraka and Lyah.

Charles Joiner looked at them and said, "Ase, family. How are you doing, brother? I hope you are having a great day, my beautiful sister. My name is Charles Joiner. My friends call me CJ."

Baraka nodded his head at Charles Joiner and said, "Hotep and Ase to you, brother. We are good. What's happening with you?"

"Hotep, cool brother. What is your name?"

"I am Baraka Asari-Dokubo, and my wife's name is Lyah Asari-Dokubo."

"Where are you all from?"

"Where are you from, Mo (Uptown slang for friend)?"

"I am from BX, the Bronx. I grew up in Webster projects (Daniel Webster House)."

"Me and my husband are from right here in Uptown Harlem."

"I am feeling good. I don't know if you all are aware, but several groups are setting up our instruments and DJ musical equipment to have a night concert here on sacred grounds in Marcus Garvey Park, for a Musical Afrocentric Concert."

Lyah looked at Charles and asked, "What time is the concert going to start?"

"I started the Musical Afrocentric Concert to honor revolutionary brothers and sisters like Larry Davis, Sojourner Truth, Sonny Carson, Harriet Tubman, and William Still. We are going to continue the concert honoring our mothers of Jazz, Bedford-Stuyvesant's own Lena Horne and Harlemite,

Diahann Carroll. My goal is to always honor our elders. The DJ is setting up their turntable and sound systems, doing scratching on some ill records right now for the DJ contest that will start around 6:00 pm. Many groups and crews from all five boroughs of New York, New Jersey, Pennsylvania, Detroit, Chicago, New Orleans, Atlanta, California, and other parts of the West Coast, as well as throughout the African diaspora, are already gathering around Marcus Garvey Park. We are celebrating the originality of the fusion of African folktales with drumbeats, musical instruments, singing, dancers of all kinds, poets, graphic artists, and all that love music will be here tapping into the energy made famous at Congo Square in New Orleans, Louisiana. We are trying to recreate the energy of the Afrocentric theme of unity."

"That sounds great. I know the whole park is going to be full of the energy of our ancestors."

"We are going to attempt to master mixing the art of B-boys and B-girls, breaking, energizing the cypher of the flow, uniting the crowd as one. If the park becomes too full, we are planning to take the celebration into the streets."

"We definitely going to represent."

"I really appreciate it if you, Lyah and Baraka, stick around. We will have vendors setting up food and merchandise for the crowd that will be gathering to listen to smooth and classic music in the park."

"That sounds nice, brother Charles. We will be there at the concert."

"Alright, I'll let you beautiful people enjoy the rest of the day. It's always wonderful to see a Black Man and a Black woman together in love. I hope to see you all later at the Musical Afrocentric concert."

Charles Joiner continued walking around Marcus Garvey Park, introducing himself to people and promoting the night of the Musical Afrocentric concert. Baraka and Lyah looked around the park, feeling the smooth breeze of the wind blowing against their rich, golden melanin skin.

Lyah smiled, saying, "The concert sounds like it's going to be dope."

"I love that the concert is going to mix the fusion of historical culture and music," Baraka replied.

"The months are going by so fast. I remember January 14; I was coming home from work, and it was snowing heavily. I couldn't see my feet on the ground as I was walking home. Now the summer breeze is kissing my skin. Baraka, do you wish it was summer in Harlem all year round?"

"Yeah, July is just around the corner. That reminds me, I have to pay the property taxes on the house on July 1. It seems like the property taxes go up every year."

"Baraka, don't stress yourself out. Just use our joint savings account to pay the property taxes."

"This is going to be the last time we use our savings account to pay bills. We have to save for our future together; we cannot keep using our savings account." Baraka paused.

"Lyah, we can't keep living like this. It seems the more we pay, the more we owe."

"You are right."

Lyah placed her arm under Baraka's arm, holding his right bicep, feeling the power of his muscle. Lyah looked into Baraka eyes, feeling his energy.

He balled up his fists. "I take my warrior mindset everywhere I go; I fear no man. I am motivated for us to succeed! I've worked too hard and too long, I am determined in my purpose to win. I will do whatever I have to do to protect and provide for my family."

"I know we cannot keep living our lives like our dreams don't exist. Baraka, have faith; it's going to get better for us after you open your own photography and art school. We are winning. Real soon, I will be opening my own fashion designer boutique."

"Lyah, you always know how to make me smile. Lyah, do you know how beautiful you are? You are glowing."

"Thank you for noticing."

"I have always noticed your alluring beauty. Lyah, trust and believe, the Kemetic Goddess Aset has healed your Universal Womb."

"Baraka, you are absolutely right; my Universal Womb has healed. I have so many scars in my heart that I must allow myself to heal from. There is no need for me to blame myself any further for the miscarriages or for Mutulu being born stillborn. I know now Mutulu will forever live inside of you and my Ka (Souls). I must move forward, placing more faith into my prayers to a higher power that created me rather than trusting only in myself. I affirm my faith in the anointed Medu Neter language that I speak to Mother Creator and Father Creator, knowing they created me in a desirable perfect image with a new audacity with the balance of Akhu of Ma'at that lives within us."

"Lyah, sitting here with you, I thank you for meri (loving) me. I feel the weight of suffering release from our Ka (Souls)."

"Baraka, thank you for meri (loving) me unconditionally."

Baraka waited patiently to surprise Lyah with a gift. He stood behind her, kissing her neck as he placed a purple-colored diamond necklace Ankh around Lyah's neck. Then, he walked in front of her, bending to his knees and placing two Ankh ankle bracelets on her ankles.

He stood to his feet and asked Lyah to place an Ankh necklace around his neck. Lyah smiled with joy and excitement, kissing Baraka passionately and placing the matching purple Ankh necklaces around his neck.

Lyah and Baraka looked up, facing the sky feeling the immense presence of the Universe interconnecting their destiny to positive energy flowing around them to give rebirth to the spirit of Sadiki (faithfulness) in their Ka to continue again to have children of their own.

Lyah looked at Baraka and said, "Baraka, we should magnetically challenge our spirits tonight. To awaken a new spirit to dance for our lives."

Baraka responded, "Lyah, you are my Lah (Moon) in human form. We need to make an affirmation of our Sadiki (faithful) commitment to strengthen our future together."

Lyah and Baraka stood, holding each other's hands, saying affirmations.

"I am a husband, I am a father, I am prosperous, I am a powerful man, I am a vessel of Ra (Sun), I am truth, and I am a spiritual warrior."

"I am a wife, I am a mother, I am lovable, I am worthy to be sacred, I am magnificently beautiful, I am mystic, and I am a divine deity of life."

Baraka and Lyah started dancing with each other to the sounds of their laughter flowing in the wind.

Lyah began to feel weak and dizzy, and she fainted, falling to the ground, her breath coming slowly. Baraka quickly started performing CPR on her as Lyah's eyes closed, and she fainted in and out of consciousness. Lyah's eyes remained closed, and she was unresponsive. Baraka held Lyah's hands as she lay in his arms.

"Lyah, you were my Lah (Moon). I will always meri (love) you. You have to open your eyes now!"

Fearing for Lyah's life, Baraka began to pray to Neter as he quickly lifted Lyah into his arms, rushing her to the hospital.

A few hours later, Lyah awoke, laying in a hospital bed, unsure of what had happened to her. Baraka remained by her side with tears in his eyes, praying to Neter for her. Lyah's physicians entered her hospital room, reviewing her medical chart with smiles on their faces. One of the physicians looked at Baraka and spoke to him.

"Baraka, I hope your tears are of joy? Because Lyah is in perfect health. Congratulations to you both, Lyah, you are pregnant!"

"What! I am what? I am pregnant!"

"Yes, you are two months pregnant!"

Lyah looked at Baraka with excitement, reaching out her left arm for him to hold her hand. He grabbed hold of both of her arms, kissing the palms of her hands.

"Baraka, you heard what the doctor said? Wow… We waited for a long time. We are finally going to have a family of our own!"

"My beautiful meri Lah (Moon), I heard what he said."

"I heard you confessing your meri (Love) for me. You are Ra (Sun)!"

Lyah and Baraka were overjoyed by the exciting news of their lives being reborn through the creation of the baby forming in Lyah's Universal Womb. They began to hug and kiss each other, knowing that Neter (Most Highest Creators) was answering their prayers with new life within their anointed marriage. After leaving the hospital, Lyah listened carefully to her physician and holistic doula's instructions to ensure a safe and healthy pregnancy. Baraka applied olive oil to Lyah's womb every night while she slept.

Lyah and Baraka attended each doctor's appointment, remaining strong in their faith of having their first healthy child. The intimacy of their bond of love immersed them, connecting them to each other throughout the months of Lyah's pregnancy.

The faithfulness of their prayers was received by Neter (Most Highest Creators) for a divine purpose within Lyah and Baraka's life. Holy blessings of the ninth month of rebirth of life had begun.

On November 10, 2022, Lyah awoke to the sound of thunderous rain outside. She glanced at the clock and noticed that it was 7:37 am in the morning. Lyah began to feel labor pains as her water broke. She wanted to make sure there was no unnecessary bleeding to be alarmed over. After checking, she didn't notice or feel any unnecessary blood coming from her Universal Womb. She then took a deep breath, feeling water coming down her thighs and legs. She woke up Baraka to share the news of her labor pains. He asked Lyah if she was okay, and she assured him she was fine.

Baraka quickly helped Lyah get dressed before dressing himself. He called a taxicab for him and Lyah. He picked up a luggage bag he had prepared days before to take with them to the hospital. With patience, he walked Lyah down their brownstone steps to catch a taxi to the hospital's emergency room. The taxi driver's name was Drexler, and he sped down the street, finally arriving at the hospital's emergency department entrance. Baraka and the taxi driver assisted

Lyah out of the taxi. Baraka noticed a wheelchair in the lobby area and rushed inside to grab it. He placed Lyah into the wheelchair and reached into his pocket, handing Drexler thirty dollars, saying, "Ayo, my man, we appreciate you. Keep the change!"

The medical staff then escorted them to the labor and delivery department. Lyah had been in labor for twenty hours and twenty-two minutes when she was settled into her hospital room. Baraka, holding an Ankh symbol over her womb, prayed for the holistic creation of life through her Universal Womb.

Lyah's holistic doula arrived and began rubbing olive oil on Lyah's womb. Baraka held Lyah's left hand to provide comfort as she grappled with pain, sweat, and exhaustion that overwhelmed her Universal Womb.

Suddenly, she felt a surge of power within her spirit, strengthening her divine feminine energy throughout her body. Despite the increasing sweat and exhaustion, she continued to push, inhaling and exhaling as the pain persisted.

Hours turned into minutes, and she closed her eyes, feeling sweat dripping into them. With another deep breath, she heard the cry of her baby, filling her and Baraka's Ka (Souls) with excitement. Lyah's OB/GYN physician urged her, "Don't stop now. Keep pushing! Keep pushing!"

Lyah and Baraka welcomed their son into the world at 4:47 am on November 11, 2022. Lyah began to cry tears of deep emotional love for her son. The physician handed Baraka surgical sterile scissors to cut the umbilical cord from the placenta, disconnecting Lyah's placenta. Baraka nervously cut the cord and then watched as the physician handed their newborn baby to Lyah. She cradled him in her arms, kissing his forehead and chest, and offering prayers for his Spirit, Soul, and physical form. She stared at her newborn son in amazement, rendered speechless.

Baraka took a seat next to Lyah as she lay in the hospital bed, and they marveled at the spiritual creation of their son. Hours passed since Lyah had given birth, and her assigned nurse entered the room, informing Lyah that it was time to breastfeed her baby boy. Lyah laid in bed and breastfed him, offering a prayer of thanksgiving to Neter. With tears in her eyes, she kept kissing her newborn baby, saying, "My handsome prince, you are my greatest grand rising! Grand Rising, I meri you so much! Welcome home, my adored little warrior prince!"

Baraka proudly stood to his feet and gazed outside the hospital room window. He looked up at the sky, where a spiritual rainbow intimately connected to Ra (Sun) appeared. Turning around, he stared into Lyah's eyes and smiled, saying with deep spiritual consciousness, "Yeah, I am feeling myself. Back on my Kemetic square with my queen and my prince. Life is good. I am so amazed by the gift of life we share together, Lyah! Ra has the ability to conquer any challenge we face in our Ka (Souls)."

"Words cannot express how bless and enchanted my heart is feeling right now! I Meri (Love) you, Baraka and our prince."

"You are my newest Grand Rising my prince. You were born on 11-11-2022. 11/11 means manifestation, new beginning, prosperity and gift!'

Baraka looked at Lyah, smiling. He kissed her belly after she gave birth. "Lyah, you are my favorite forever meri (love) story. This is the grandest rising in my Spirit I've ever experience. Thank you, my Queen of Lah (Queen Moon) for your life and for our prince. I am so proud of you my queen! You have given birth to our harvest of thanksgiving to Neter!"

"You will always be my Ra (Sun). I am the daughter of Queen of Lah, anointed with gifts of giver of birth through my Universal Nu (Black) womb of life. I am honored to carry ancient Ka (Souls) from my ancestral mother womb!'

Baraka kissed Lyah's lips softly. He then cradled a part of his Ka (Soul) in his arms as he held his son close. Baraka heard the echo of his voice in his son's cry. He stared at his prince's face, seeing a reflection of himself and Lyah's Ka (Souls) mirrored in their son's features. Suddenly, without hesitation, Baraka and Lyah looked outside the window and witnessed a falcon soaring powerfully in the spirit of the heavenly skies.

He continued to gaze outside, raising his noble prince toward the heavens, and speaking his son's noble Nubian Kemetic warrior names into existence, addressing Neter (Most

Highest Creator Gods and Goddesses) and all the Holy Spirits of their ancestors. In the middle of the night, Lyah lay in the hospital bed, feeling exhausted from giving birth. She reached out her hands as Baraka placed Taharqa Ausar Asari-Dokuba against her chest. She continued breastfeeding him, strengthening their bond as mother queen Lyah.

She purified her desire to express her love for her prince, Taharqa, as he opened his mouth, yawning and stretching out his body to claim his existence in the ma'at. Taharqa felt his mother's heartbeat, finding calmness in his Ka (Soul) as she nursed him with the rich organic nutrients of her breast milk. She whispered into his ear how much she loved and cherished him.

Lyah and Baraka took turns holding their prince Taharqa Ausar Asari-Dokubo, gently squeezing him with tears of joy in their eyes. Lyah kissed her baby boy on his forehead, tears of love falling from her eyes. She was mesmerized, holding him in her arms, feeling blessed for the gift of life she and Baraka had received. Lyah spent the night talking and singing to Taharqa, songs her parents had sung to her when she was a young girl. Moments passed without notice within Lyah's Ka (Soul) as she prayed to the Most High Creator, giving thanks for the harvest of Taharqa to her Spirit.

The divine flow of Spiritual energy captivated Baraka and Lyah Asari-Dokubo's Souls, united with the birth of their prince, bestowing his spirit with the holy name Taharqa Ausar Asari-Dokubo. When Lyah fell asleep, Baraka held his prince

Taharqa Ausar Asari-Dokubo tightly in his arms. He spoke to him while looking out of the hospital window, lifting Taharqa up to the heavens, reflecting on an inspirational book he had read about the Zulu oath declaration of the Zulu Nation of People. Baraka stared into the mirror of the Ka of his prince Taharqa Ausar Asari-Dokubo, saying...

"I am, you are. I am essence. Our son, you're mother queen, and I want you to always know these words exist within your Ka (Soul)."

"I am, I am. I will always step forward with my left leg and then my right leg to gain a greater understanding of my purpose to our Divine Creator and my ancestral divinity that unites me with a Universal Global Family of Nu (Black) People."

When I was growing up, I chased after Ra to find my essence, but you showed me the Spirit of Ra was always within me. Hotep, my prince Taharqa Ausar Asari-Dokubo, you are my new beginning! Ungawa, Ungawa, Ungawa to the Black family. On the move! I am on the move with my divine queen goddess, Lyah, and our divine prince, Taharqa Ausar Asari-Dokubo!"

Acknowledgments

Paul Mark (Ra"ShyAlah Sakura the Poet) is the author of a thought-provoking novel, The Genocide of Hip-Hop (The Cry of Blood), that was published in 2012. Ra'ShyAlah Sakura continued his desire and passion for a greater understanding of the history of the spiritual spirit of the Afrikan diaspora.

In 2016, Paul Mark, and fifty other Nu (Black) People embarked on a spiritual pilgrimage (Kemet Nu (Black) know thyself Tour) with Baba Ashra and Mother Merira Kwesi. His spiritual journey through Kemet transformed Ra'SyAlah Sakura the Poet's life forever. When he arrived in Kemet (Egypt) he felt right at home, knowing he was walking on sacred soil. This land was built and created thousands of years ago by the Most Highest Creator and Ra'ShyAlah Sakura's ancestors. Several times while visiting the pyramids and temples in Kemet (Egypt), Ra'ShyAlah Sakura bent down blowing love kisses, praying to the Most Highest Creator. He felt the anointed spiritual, and powerful balance of Ra (Sun) and Lah (Moon) guiding his path with each day throughout the Spiritual Enlightenment of the holy land of Kemet. At the conclusion of his pilgrimage, he knew his divine purpose was connecting him to his path of cultural freedom. Tears embraced his heart and soul promising his spirit he would continue writing the history of his Ancestral homeland.

About the Author

Ra'ShyAlah Sakura, known as The Poet, is a multifaceted artist based in Manhattan, New York City. Engaged in the performing arts scene, he has been an integral part of the Barrow Group Performing Arts Center Theater Company since 2018, honing his craft through playwriting and theater acting classes. His journey in the world of spoken word began in 1997, and it has been a continuous passion in his artistic repertoire.

As an accomplished author, Ra'ShyAlah Sakura has left his mark with the publication of *The Genocide of Hip-Hop (The Cry of Blood)*, available on Amazon. His literary achievements extend to winning the Age of Innocence poetry contest in 2001 and writing three books. With a deep commitment to storytelling, he expanded his reach by starting the website "Ancient Voices of Spirituality" from 2013 to 2017, ensuring his narratives resonate globally.

Beyond the realm of literature, Ra'ShyAlah Sakura is a dynamic playwright and screenwriter, with three plays and two movies slated for future release. His dedication to the craft is evident through participation in various writing workshops across Connecticut, New York City, and California. Notably, he has been a part of influential events such as the Black Writers on Tour and the Word to Everything Creative Writing Workshop in 2019.

Ra'ShyAlah Sakura's artistic pursuits are deeply intertwined with community activism. In Hartford, CT, and Newark, NJ, he collaborates with activists to address youth-related issues, including feeding the homeless and counseling against violence and substance abuse. His commitment extends to financial donations and providing free educational books to foster cultural awareness. Through his poems, novels, plays, and screenplays, Ra'ShyAlah Sakura strives to inspire pride in the ancient history of Black communities worldwide, urging them to look beyond the physical lens and explore the vastness of their Universal Souls. His upcoming works promise to authentically portray the African diaspora, contributing to a richer narrative in motion pictures and on stage.

www.ingramcontent.com/pod-product-compliance
Lightning Source LLC
Chambersburg PA
CBHW022003120726

47992CB00001B/386